Diving for Poems

by

David Kirby

Word Beat Press

Grateful acknowledgement is made to the following publications for permission to reprint poems in this volume.

Apalachee Quarterly: "Coconuts, Plane Crashes, and Mangos"

Carolina Quarterly: "The Dance of Husbands in Bathrobes"

Chelsea: "Patience"

City Lights Books: lines from "America," "A Step Away From Them"

Michigan Quarterly Review: "The Doctor of Starlight"

New Collage: "Hitchhiking in France"

New Statesman: "Nuns at Birth"

New Yorker: "Tropical Fish"

Poetry: "The Crybaby at the Library," "My Cat Jack"

Southern Poetry Review: "Letter to Borges"

The following poems appeared in my book *Sarah Bernhardt's Leg*, published by the Cleveland State University Poetry Center: "The Bear," "Dracula's Bride," "How to Use This Body," "In the Dark There Are Shapes Everywhere," "Saving the Young Men of Vienna," "Sub Rosa," "To My Sons," and "The Visible Man."

The introduction, "Why We Need a Million Poets," appeared in different form in the March, 1984 issue of *College English*.

Thanks to Little, Brown and to the Society of Jesus and Oxford University Press respectively for permission to reprint copyrighted poems by Emily Dickinson and Gerard Manley Hopkins.

Thanks to Dale Loucareas for permission to print in different form her guidelines for submitting poems in Appendix B.

Thanks to George Anderson, Mary Ann Farrell, Glenn Marsh, David Morris, Sandra Sprayberry, David Trimble, and Charles Vignos for permission to print their work. They and students like them also taught me what to say about poetry.

Special thanks to Allen Woodman for suggesting that I write this book in the first place.

Cover Illustration by David Sheskin

Library of Congress Number: 85-050496

ISBN: 0-912527-03-X

Word Beat Press
Post Office Box 10509
Tallahassee, Florida 32302

for William and Ian

Table of Contents

Introduction

WHY WE NEED A MILLION POETS

The first university English departments taught little except literature, which was usually divided into historical periods: the Eighteenth-Century Novel, American Literature After World War I. But in the late 1960s, the mission of English departments was altered forever by sheer demographics. The baby boomers, made confident by a new music, new forms of sexual expression, and new ways of altering the consciousness, had better things to do than read literary masterpieces. On campus the disaffected young showed less interest in traditional literature and more interest in creative writing, women's studies, and minority studies. Of these three, minority studies seems to have diminished in popularity in recent years, and the interest in women's studies has stabilized; only creative writing seems to have continued to grow.

While this growth is good news for administrators concerned about a sag in English enrollments among an increasingly job-oriented student body, not all of the faculty is happy. After all, creative writing is ahistorical in nature. It is anti-hierarchical. It denies the validity of a monopoly viewpoint. Finally, creative writing promotes a distinctly unscholarly way of viewing literature. In *Against Interpretation*, Susan Sontag writes, "In place of hermeneutics [that is, a science of interpretation] we need an erotics of art." Meaning be damned, says the poet, let's see how the text *feels*.

The surge in creative writing has had a marked effect on the teaching of traditional English courses, and today more literature teachers than before are using the methods of the writing workshop— frequent short assignments, peer criticism, individual conferences— as opposed to the lecture/text/term paper approach. This influence is in general a beneficial one, because unless it is designed with extraordinary care, a traditional test or term paper is fated to be a dilution of someone else's expertise, either the teacher's or a critic's or

7

David Kirby

both. The student goes over the class notes, reads a book on the subject (most likely the first one he or she sees in the card catalog), and brings the arguments down to the level of a nineteen- or twenty-year-old. This student is encouraged to begin in wisdom and move away from it. By contrast, the *sine qua non* of all imaginative writing is the ignorance in which all writers begin, the problem which the world sets for them and which they must solve. No poem ever began with an answer. Thirteen hundred and twelve lines into *Song of Myself*, Walt Whitman is still saying, "I do not know it—it is without name—it is a word unsaid."

Creative writing can be taught badly, of course. The worst approach, yet one used with distressing frequency, is that of self-expression. A more honorable approach, yet by no means the best, is one that advocates the creation of a purely verbal construct, a poem that is self-sufficient and seductive, even if it does not point beyond itself; unfortunately, this sometimes results in a "workshop poem" which says nothing but says it elegantly. The most fruitful approach sees writing as a means to more acute vision—as a way to solve problems, if there are problems to be solved, but also a method of increasing mental and emotional agility, an athletics of the spirit, as it were. When you link convincingly two unrelated objects or ideas, or when you follow something to its logical conclusion and then push past logic into meaningful *non sequitur*, you are doing what you came to the university to do in the first place, not to get vocational training but to think and feel in fresh and original ways, with heart and mind working together. Far from being the impractical major, English teaches a passionate yet detached way of seeing the world. In this way the student of English becomes like the little heroine of Henry James's *What Maisie Knew*, her nose flattened against "the hard window-pane of the sweetshop of knowledge." No wonder so many university administrators are former English professors; no wonder more corporations are increasing their hiring of liberal-arts majors over ones who have elected "practical" concentrations yet have never learned to think. A recent issue of the professional journal *College English* contains an article on the importance of poetry to pre-law students; both poems and legal cases involve the assembling of materials, the selection of a single approach from among the several that suggest themselves, and so on.

In writing *Diving for Poems*, I have been much influenced by the imaginative thinking that lies behind the Poets in the Schools program and such books for schoolchildren as Kenneth Koch's *Wishes, Lies, and Dreams*. Poems are not found on the surface of life. The poet must dive deeply for them, and consequently many poems are subversions of the educational and personal status quo. With young children, teachers often have to insist that students forget themselves while writing or that they don't have to tell the truth or that they can even record their "rotten" thoughts. How different all this is from the sunny, vitamin-enriched, one-dimensional world that teaches only surfaces, never depths! Henry James complained that his brother William wanted him to write novels according to the two-and-two-make-four system for people who were incapable of seeing the world in any other way. Two and two do make four, but they also make twenty-two, a much bigger number.

"Thinking is involuntary," said Buckminster Fuller; "you do or you don't." Most writing, which is only patterned thinking, after all, is equally involuntary. Almost all professional writers began writing when they were children, feel bad when they go for long periods without writing, and so on. If this is so, what justification is there for teaching writing to hundreds of thousands of students who have never done it before with any seriousness and who, in all likelihood, will never do it again? There can be only one answer, and it is that imaginative writing, conducted at a high level, is one path leading to the back door of knowledge. The "practical" way, the way of received knowledge and "common sense," is the way of robots. The two-and-two-make-four system leads to shabby thinking in everything from literature to foreign policy. Good writing is good reading is good thinking: it's playful and engaged, passionate and detached at one and the same time. And yes, it can be taught.

The first part of this book deals with the raw material of poetry, and the second part deals with the shaping of that material into finished poems. As examples I use poems by well-known authors but also ones by my students and myself. While poems from the latter group may never attain the celebrity of those by Gerard Manley Hopkins and Emily Dickinson, I use them nonetheless because I know where they came from and how they were changed along the way.

Part One
WHAT IS POETRY?

When Boswell asked Johnson, "What is poetry?"
Johnson answered: "Why, Sir, it is much easier
to say what it is not. We all know what light is;
but it is not easy to tell what it is."

Paul Fussell, Jr.

Take care of the sounds, and the sense will
take care of itself.

Lewis Carroll

What a Poem is Not

At one of his first poetry readings, the young Robert Frost found himself being heckled by an old-timer sitting in the front row. Every time Frost finished reading a poem, his tormentor would say, "Do you call that poetry?" Frost survived the ordeal, of course, and his poems endure. Unfortunately, an antipathy to contemporary poetry still exists as well. That antipathy can be heard in statements like "the last real poet was Yeats" and "you can't tell me this Ginsberg fellow is a poet." These are partially learned statements, of course; at least they show some knowledge of literature. More common and more disconcerting is the unhappy wail of the student who is coerced into reading and perhaps even writing free verse for the first time: "I thought poetry had to rhyme!"

This student probably got that idea from a harried schoolteacher who, trying to preside over an overcrowded classroom of hormone-driven adolescents, must make things black and white if order is to be preserved and information imparted. Thus prose is the stuff that doesn't rhyme, poetry the stuff that does. This is a partially true statement, but so is a statement like "all human beings are male." Many human beings are not male, and many poems are unrhymed. In fact, most of the poems written in the last hundred years have not had rhyme, meter, or formal structure. So while a statement like "the last real poet was Yeats" may reveal an affection for one of the great artists of our culture, it also reveals a savage bigotry, an arrogant disdain for the splendid poems that have been written since Yeats' day.

With some significant exceptions, then, most of the poems that are being written today are not characterized primarily by rhyme or a fixed metrical scheme or a set number of lines. The problem is that it is so much easier to list what a poem is not than to say what a poem is that one is tempted to fall back on the old reliable (and only partly facetious) definition of a contemporary poem: a poem is the literary form whose lines need not extend all the way to the right-hand margin.

There is actually a lot of hidden truth in this playful definition, however. The point is that the poetic form today must be free to do what other contemporary literary genres and the poetry of the past cannot do. Recently I asked a class to read some contemporary poems; I discussed the individual poems in detail but I did not provide any sort of theory, and when we were finished, I posed the following question: "What good is poetry?" One student wrote, "Poetry can say things that other literary genres would have a hard time saying—rhythm, images, diction all help to convey underlying thoughts." The key word here is "underlying," since the compression of most poems guarantees a greater proportion of subterranean material than is normally found in a story or play, for example, where plot and dramatic action dominate. A good poem burrows under the surface.

A second student wrote that "poetry evokes mental images which seem to unlock thoughts that were previously being suppressed for one reason or another." Because we don't know what these thoughts are before we think them consciously, we cannot unearth them by simply using some tried-and-true method that has always worked; this fact alone accounts for the dazzling variety of poem types which have appeared in the last hundred years.

A third student wrote, "I feel that because there are no rules about the structure of a poem that the author can say exactly what he feels in any way that he feels like saying it." (Wisely, this same person wrote, "I'm not saying that I like all poetry and that all poetry is good and wonderful.")

Finally, one student said that "poetry is good for people who can look past the paper and the ink." If there is nothing on the other side of the paper and the ink, of course, then there is no poem.

A Poem Is a Journey

Each poem is a journey that, like any other, entertains and edifies. First the poet embarks, then the reader. The going is usually more difficult for the poet, who makes false starts, wrong turns, and premature halts, although the reader should expect to stumble as well. Indeed, part of the pleasure of any journey we take is in the stumbling, at least in retrospect—you remember how you barely caught the train or ordered a meal in sign language as the waiter in the Greek restaurant rolled his eyes and sighed. As with any trip, there are some known elements which supply security and many more unknown elements which account for the adventure. No poem should be praised because it is easy to understand. A traffic sign and a menu should be easy to understand; they deal with the world of surfaces and must be readily comprehensible if they are to fulfill their functions. But not a poem. Writing of some recent Spanish poetry, the critic Andrew Debicki makes a statement that applies to the poetry of every country when he says that a poem is "a vehicle for a creative but necessarily incomplete journey of discovery, a journey in which both speaker and reader participate and in which the language of the text does not always provide definitive answers." In fact, a poem may not provide answers at all.

The poet A. R. Ammon offers an attractive version of the poem-as-journey metaphor. To Ammons, a poem is like a walk.

First, both a poem and a walk involve the whole person, says Ammons. A poem is more than a mental activity, since we see, feel, and hear in it the poet's own bodily rhythms and sense of physical relationship to—or separation from—the world. As we read, we add our own smiles, gasps, and cluckings. We may even leap to our feet in amazed delight or sink down into despair.

Second, both a poem and a walk are unreproducible. You cannot take the same walk twice; the air will be different, the trees will have changed, the people you meet will not be the ones you met before. You cannot write the same poem twice or even read it twice—one of the great pleasures of rereading is the discovery in a poem of elements you did not notice before.

Third, each turns and returns. A good poem or walk always ventures into new territory but then safely sees the writer or reader or walker home again. It is sometimes said that every good poem argues with itself, just as a walk is "arguing" when it leads the walker up the new street or into the woods and then back to the beaten path.

Finally, poems and walks are both characteristic of their makers. How often do you hear someone say, "I can tell that walk from a mile away" or "I knew that was you by the way you walk"? Just as there are characteristic ways of walking that can only be identified intuitively, so we can say, often without knowing why, "This is a poem by Poet X—or at least it isn't by Poet Y."

Learning to write in a manner that is characteristic of our true selves is like learning to walk; it takes time, and there will be plenty of missteps. But we will end up going places we have never been before, places we did not even know existed.

Where Does Poetry Come From?

You do not need to know where poetry comes from in order to be able to write a good poem. But a successful career in any field is bound to be plagued with moments of doubt and despair, and at those moments it is comforting to know that at least one is proceeding correctly. Even when things are going well, it is encouraging to know why they are going well and to understand also that productivity has its limits; that way, when dry periods come along (and they will, no matter how accomplished one is), it helps to know that this is natural too and that one can at least look forward to the fruitful period to come. The failure to understand the workings of their own minds may be the reason behind the self-destructive behavior of so many artists.

The brain has always been described in terms of the image that dominates the age. In the long agricultural period that makes up most of human history, the brain was described as a field to be enriched by wholesome activities and edifying literature. With Freud's discovery of the unconscious, the brain became a steam engine, the dominant image of the Industrial Revolution. Today we think of the brain as being like a computer, something that can be programmed, and this leads us to think differently about the brain's functions. In Freud's day, for example, anger had to be released; if the operator of the steam engine failed to relieve the pressure, the engine might explode. Today, of course, we see self-expression as a form of programming, and therefore excessive expressions of anger are to be avoided—all you will end up with is an angry computer.

From the point of view of creativity, perhaps it is best to think of the brain as a hotel. Here we find both horizontal and vertical activity. Some doors are opened, some are closed. People arrive and depart, bearing all sorts of luggage. In this room there is passionless sex, in this one genuine love. On the floor below a business deal has just been consummated. There is quiet conversation in the new wing—and in the penthouse, murder! And always there is someone cleaning up.

Recent findings in neurophysiology suggest that this hotel image is a fairly accurate one. In the proportion of its various parts, the brain is like an orange: the central part is the pulp or medulla, a prolongation

16

of the spinal cord, and the outer portion is the rind or cortex. The cortex itself has three divisions: the archicortex or reptilian brain; the mesocortex or early mammalian brain; and the neocortex or later mammalian brain. The interesting thing about the cortex is that it was simply added onto during the process of evolution, whereas other body parts changed completely; flippers became arms, for example, and gills turned into lungs.

Each of the three cortices has a different function. The reptile brain rather coldly tends to such matters of survival as obtaining food. The early mammalian brain is passionate and thus capable of both anger and sexual love. And the later mammalian brain is responsible for such higher functions as contemplation and insight. So what we call "the brain" is really three brains. Physiologist Paul Maclean asks us to imagine "that when the psychiatrist bids the patient to lie on a couch, he is asking him to stretch out alongside a horse and a crocodile," noting that it is "little wonder that the patient who has personal responsibility for these animals and who must serve as their mouthpiece is sometimes accused of being full of resistance and reluctant to talk."

In addition to these three divisions, the neocortex or later mammalian brain is further divided into left and right hemispheres. The left hemisphere is concerned with logic and analysis, while the right hemisphere is the seat of intuition and nonverbal perception. Somewhat confusingly, the rational left hemisphere governs the right side of the body, whereas the intuitive right hemisphere controls the left or "sinister" side (the French word *sinistre* means "left") and accounts for a longlived suspicion of the left-handed. The two hemispheres do communicate, of course; the dreamy right hemisphere is constantly muttering to the wide-awake left hemisphere by means of a nerve pathway called the anterior commissure.

Similarly, the three cortices are in contact with one another. People with poor mental control are prone to such emotional problems as paranoia, which stems from unregulated activity in the archicortex; in the absence of real enemies, the reptile brain will invent imaginary ones so that it has something to conquer. On the other hand, improved mental control over the mind can lead to creativity. Arthur Koestler, whose own numerous and varied books are a staggering testament to the powers of the mind, notes that "poetry could...be said to achieve a synthesis between the sophisticated reasoning of the neocortex and the more primitive emotional ways of the old brain." Since we do not spend all day in a single cortex or a single hemisphere of the neocortex but flip back and forth constantly from one to

David Kirby

another, the secret is to be aware of the flips, to bring the deep ancestral images of the reptile brain and the fiery passions of the early mammalian brain up into the well-lit chambers of the new brain, where they can be tested both logically and intuitively, examined, sequenced, and revised.

The Vatic Voice

Within each of us is something called the vatic voice. *Vates* is a Greek word which means the inspired poet, the poet speaking the words of a god. To most people the vatic voice speaks only in dreams. But the vatic voice is also the source of all art.

It is the vatic voice which speaks when energy is transferred from the archicortex or mesocortex to the neocortex, or from the right hemisphere of the neocortex to the left. Different writers trigger that transfer in different ways. Hart Crane sometimes stimulated the flow of poetic images by listening to the music of Ravel played very loud. Gertrude Stein is said to have written at Parisian intersections with all the horns blaring behind her. Donald Hall believes in the benefits of short naps: "There is that wonderful long, delicious slide or drift down heavy air to the bottom of sleep, which you touch only for a moment, and then there is the floating up again, more swiftly, through an incredible world of images, sometimes in bright colors."

Poets often speak of the benefits of boredom in writing poetry. Here is Philip Levine, for example:

I don't so nearly search for my poems as they find me. I don't run away from them. Which is what I see some people do. I mean, there's no way the poem is going to find you if you're playing ping-pong. Or cha-cha-cha-ing. Chasing girls, or whatever it is you chase. Perfecting your back stroke. I mean, there's no way. You have to be there. In some state of readiness and hospitality to the fucking muse, you know, who is, after all, only a part of you. You have to let it open the door and come into your brain, into your hand, wherever it comes. And I do a lot of that. I mean I sit lots of hours picking my nose. I don't even pick my nose. I do nothing. I've learned that you have to do nothing. You have to be silent and see if the voice will enter you.

I once asked a class of experienced poets, several of whom had been widely published, how they encouraged the vatic voice. Many of them

18

said that ideas for poems came during classes and lectures, while attending church services or other formal functions, while driving or watching a bad movie. Some students said that reading was useful; one often becomes impatient and then competitive ("I can write a better poem than this"). Poetry readings have stimulated a lot of poems, both because they inspire competitive feelings and because they can be very boring at times. Some students meditated, usually in a non-religious manner of the type described in Herbert Benson's little book *The Relaxation Response.*

Of course these are all ways of getting bored and encouraging the flow of images. Going back to the physiology of the brain, Robert Bly puts it this way: "If the body sits in a room for an hour, quietly, doing nothing, the reptile brain becomes increasingly restless. It wants excitement, danger.... If the sitter continues the mammal brain quickly becomes restless too. It wants excitement, confrontations, insults, sexual joy. It now starts to feed in spectacular erotic imagery, of the sort that St. Anthony's sittings were famous for. Yet if the sitter persists in doing nothing, eventually energy has nowhere to go but the new brain." All the poet has to do then, as Philip Levine says, is be there.

As far as other methods of stimulating the vatic voice are concerned, one student in the class I mentioned said he depended on psychedelic mushrooms for his poetry. Interestingly, he was the worst poet of the group. I have noticed that poems sometimes come to me just after I have lit a cigar or taken the first sip of a cup of coffee or glass of beer. But less is more in a case like this: I would not get more or better images by smoking an entire box of cigars or drinking all the coffee or beer in the house, and in fact I would incapacitate myself for any creative activity at all. Experimental studies have shown that while drugged poets will have poets' visions, drugged accountants will simply have accountants' visions, and so on. If you are not a poet, no amount of artificial stimulation will help. And if you are, you may as well try boredom first. It's cheaper and easier on the metabolism.

First Drafts

Not everything uttered by the vatic voice is worth listening to. Often the image or phrase that starts the poet on the path to a finished poem is one that must be discarded. This is sometimes difficult to do;

naturally one feels loyal toward or sentimental about one's points of departure. Still, given the turns a poem is likely to take, the first image is one that may be totally incongruous by the time a poem is finished. If it doesn't threaten the whole with contamination, at best it may be superfluous. In that case the poet must mercilessly snip it off, just as the glassblower cuts away his pipe from the object he has just made.

This kind of cold manipulation of a poem is sometimes called "depersonalization." Poems are very personal to both writer and reader, but they only get that way through a process that is clear-eyed and analytical. After all, art is a child both of the animal brains and the new brains as well; total reliance on instinct is just as fatal as total reliance on logic. Freud had a wonderful understanding of how the poet uses every aspect of the brain to create a work that gives to the reader a pleasure analogous to that felt by the poet during the act of composition:

> ...to those who are not artists the gratification that can be drawn from the springs of phantasy is very limited; their inexorable repressions prevent the enjoyment of all but the meagre day-dreams which can become conscious. A true artist has more at his disposal. First of all he understands how to elaborate his day-dreams, so that they lose that personal note which grates upon strange ears and become enjoyable to others; he knows too how to modify them sufficiently so that their origin in prohibited sources is not so easily detected. Further, he possesses the mysterious ability to mould his particular material until it expresses the ideas of his phantasy faithfully; and then he knows how to attach to this reflection of his phantasy-life so strong a stream of pleasure that, for a time at least, the repressions are out-balanced and dispelled by it. When he can do all this, he opens to others the way back to the comfort and consolation of their own unconcious sources of pleasure, and so reaps their gratitude and admiration.

Notice that Freud makes only one distinction between writers and readers. Both groups have "meagre day-dreams," and writers simply take the time to make their daydreams more complex and pleasurable. The poet Donald Davie once said, "I will not trust dreams to do what only a composed fable can do," which is much the same thing. We all have dreams, and artists simply turn theirs into fables; when we read these fables, we are simply dreaming again, but this time in a sustained and exhilarating way.

If the artist has done everything correctly, that is. Davie says that "a poem is no good if something personally rather difficult—person-ally rather discreditable—isn't near the heart of it. But then the business of art is to release and utter those painful or in many cases shameful things without embarrassing the person who hears you say them.''

The following poem, written by a student, shows how depersonalization works. This person suffers from chronic pain, pain so severe it can only be treated by means of a small pump which has been implanted in her body and which drips a highly concentrated morphine solution directly onto her spinal cord. She has been in and out of hospitals all her life and undergone countless operations. In this poem she addresses one of the many nurses she has encountered, a nurse who tries in vain to comfort her the way nurses tried futilely to comfort the soldiers who were hideously mutilated in the battles of the Civil War.

A Neon Body

You hold the empty syringe
like someone in a photograph
holding a cigarette
and tell me what I have is not real,
that it only pounds in cerebral aqueducts
and hemispheres, producing warped dreams.
My only real pain, you say, has a sulphate base,
and I can have that puncture me
any time I push the call button.
In stupor I cannot reply;
I am clamped in a sleep not of my own.

Come morning I still hear your voice
and now I have that nailed smile memorized.
Nurse, nurse, go back to your forms;
your needles and dyes show nothing.
How I know those results far better than you.
Your voice is a calendar
of ignorant song.
It sweetly lipped the same words
to one-legged Rebels,
home from Bull Run,
begging something was wrong.

When pity leashed their lives,
they pulled handguns from drawers.

I've no gun, know no war.
I have an imperfect bond of perfect love.
I cling to the pity in sand:
Alone on tiny Holden's Beach
I lay before the high water
with waves making isometrics
of my useless legs. I felt the burning
orange neon
cup the nerves of hip and calf
like some cheap cocktail sign.
Sharp, scalding lines,
an electric switch shorted
before the giant ocean's current.
The moon was on my face for hours
and with each tidal cape
it was only the tiny coquina and donax
immediately finding their way home
that hot, brilliant July night.

                              MARY ANN FARRELL

Writing from the same viewpoint, almost anyone else would have tried
to recreate the pain itself and talk about how terrible it is; the result
would be an embarrassing poem, one that makes the reader
uncomfortable, a poem that might even make the reader hate the poet
for creating such an atmosphere of self-pity. Instead, in the poem I
have quoted here, it is easy to see how brave the writer is, how she has
confronted her pain and, realizing that she can never conquer it
completely, takes what solace she can from the healing waters of the
Atlantic Ocean, which massage and comfort her like a lover, like a
helpless and devoted god. Now perhaps the writer isn't anywhere near
this stoic (though I know for a fact she is), but that is not the point. In
good poetry we get a strong sense of the poet's self, but instead of
being an ordinary or spontaneous self, it is usually an improved self, a
depersonalized self. Most great art is an improved version of what
already exists, beginning with the writer's own personality.

    Depersonalization is best thought of as a matter of picking the right
words and excluding the wrong ones. Renoir once said to Mallarmé,

"You know, I have a lot of ideas that I would like to put into poems," and Mallarmé replied, "Poems are not written with ideas but with words." If you think only of putting an idea or a feeling on paper, you are very likely to end up with a vague and amorphous expression of something that is specific to you and quite meaningless to anyone else. Worse, you may strike your reader as naive or even dishonest. As F. Scott Fitzgerald says in his short story "The Rich Boy," "When I hear a man proclaiming himself an 'average, honest, open fellow,' I feel pretty sure that he has some definite and perhaps terrible abnormality to conceal—and his protestation of being average and honest and open is his way of reminding himself of his misprision." However, if you put hollow-sounding ideas aside for the moment and concentrate on selecting the right words, you are on your way to the shared fantasy that brings writer and reader together.

The first sentence of "The Rich Boy" reads like this: "Begin with an individual, and before you know it you find that you have created a type; begin with a type, and you find that you have created—nothing." Fitzgerald proceeds to build up his rich boy word by word, making him alternately attractive and repulsive, so that by the time the story ends, we feel as though we know almost everything about this particular character (the "individual") as well as a great deal about others in the same social class (the "type").

Fitzgerald gives us the general by devoting himself entirely to the specific, a process that is impossible to reverse without all meaning being lost. Consider this little disappearing act that the philosopher Jacques Barzun performs with a simple McIntosh apple:

> Take, for example, this small, hard, round red object that fills your present sight, touch, and sense of smell, and that you immediately "identify" as a McIntosh apple. By naming it you merge it with millions of similar items, each in some way different from the one in your hand. If you use only the word "apple," the concept now includes yellow and green color and possible elongated forms of unlike size and taste. *Your* apple has twice been lost sight of. If anyone goes on to speak of "a piece of fruit," the term lacks all power to compel a correct image of what is in your hand. By the time "foodstuff" is invoked, only the most general idea of function remains. Then comes "organic matter," and the next step is bare "object," at which point all things whatever are "the same."

Or how about this more homely example, which I borrow from the poet Barbara Drake? Suppose you are going to lunch and on your way you meet me, strolling contentedly and ruminating on the delicious salad I have just eaten. What would you feel if, during the course of polite conversation, I were to say, "I tell you, that salad was mighty tasty"? You would feel nothing, because I had not depersonalized my experience; through laziness or ineptitude, I am keeping it all to myself. But suppose I say this: "It was a salad of Boston lettuce, very tender, a delicate shade of green; there was feta cheese, a sprinkling of oregano and freshly ground pepper, olive oil, red-wine vinegar, and three wedges of firm, vine-ripened tomato." The process is complete. Out of my primitive desire to eat there came the need for a salad, and if you are hungry, and if you like salads at all, this description should stimulate your appetite, your own primitive desire.

The problem with an apple or a salad or even a rich boy is that it is liable to be rather ordinary in and of itself: specific, yes, even appealing in a low-grade way, but ultimately rather commonplace. How shall we make these things extraordinary, how shall we attach to them "so strong a stream of pleasure" (Freud's phrase) that they are catapulted into another, higher plane of being, and us with them? Can I describe a salad so tantalizingly that your mouth would water after you had already eaten?

This problem of putting the ordinary in an extraordinary light is one that has perplexed artists for centuries but especially in modern times, when art is less concerned with overarching belief systems and more concerned with the everyday. In this century, a group of writers and painters called the surrealists dealt with this problem in a manner that was often astonishing. Historically, surrealism was an arts movement whose works represented the breakthrough of dreams into the world of waking reality. Given its impetus by André Breton in his "Manifeste du Surréalisme" (1924) and characterized in its early days by experiments in automatic writing and drawing and other methods of evoking unconscious images, surrealism clearly owes much to the interplay between the different parts of the brain described earlier. But there is nothing abstract about the surreal, since its images are the hard-edged objects of everyday life, even though they are placed in startling juxtaposition to one another, as in a dream, say, in which a dead relative is standing on the shore of a lake which she had never visited in life. Jean-Pierre Cauvin, Breton's translator, says that "Breton is keenly aware of Freud's discovery that, in dreams, the categories of contradiction and opposition are voided, that the unconscious is blind to negation, and that dreams evince a particular tendency to join opposites together into a unit or represent them in a single object.... Characterized by immediacy and incongruence, surrealist images bypass all willful intellectual controls."

Typical of the surrealists in the visual arts is René Magritte, whose widely reproduced painting, *Le Fils d'Homme* (1964), shows a man whose face is obscured by a large green apple that seems to be floating in space. What does an apple have to do with a man? The answer to the question is "nothing," but by saying that, you have given yourself the right to say, "everything." Countless possibilities suggest themselves: that the man is a purely natural creature, like the apple, or that the apple has a kind of *élan vital* that we attribute pridefully to ourselves alone, or simply that there can be magic in our lives if we allow it to enter. Newton's apple affirmed gravity, Magritte's apple denies it. As Jean-Pierre Cauvin says, "the spark struck by the meeting of opposites clarifies by its brilliance the dullest of everyday perceptions, infusing it with the light of the marvellous."

What makes paintings worth seeing again and poems worth re-reading is the fact that new interpretations constantly suggest themselves to us. We see the painting or the poem, as André Breton says, "always for the first time" (*"toujours pour la première fois"*). Consider these lines from James Wright's poem "Spring Images":

A butterfly lights on the branch
of your green voice.

Small antelopes
Fall asleep in the ashes
Of the moon.

No matter how often one reads these lines, they will never be anything but new because their separate elements are so different—a butterfly lands on a voice, antelopes sleep on the moon—that they will always be in conflict, always presenting some argument that has not been aired before. Did James Wright know what he meant when he wrote those lines? Probably not. Another poet, Stanley Kunitz, has this to say: "Yeats taught us that out of our quarrel with others we make rhetoric; out of our quarrel with ourselves, poetry." If Wright had known what butterflies have to do with voices or antelopes with the moon, he would not have had to write his poem at all.

Logic will not be foremost in the mind of the reader, and it should not be the first concern of the writer, either. There is a real sense to a well-written poem, but it is not the sense of logic. In a marvellous essay that is itself a demonstration of how one might link two things that most people would consider entirely different, Howard Nemerov argues that a poem and a joke are pretty much the same thing. You

25

either get the joke or you do not, says Nemerov. If you do not get the joke and everyone else does, you never say that the joke is "subjective" or fails to make sense; after all, it made sense to everyone else. If you are wise, you smile politely, and if you are not, you give out a forced laugh that everyone else recognizes as fake. Should someone have to explain the joke to you, the difficulty may be cleared up, but it will be too late. You may still laugh, but not with the spontaneity of the others. Thus a poem is a way of getting something right in language, according to Nemerov, "save that the proper response will be not laughter but silence, or the acknowledgment that it is so, it is as it is; that the miracle has happened again."

Getting It Right

So far we have considered how poetry originates within us and what it sounds like when we first hear it. You know now that creative impulses begin as interactions between the different parts of the brain, and you know that the brain tends to throw to the surface all sorts of things with varying degrees of usefulness, and you know that the poet's job is to sift through these offerings, select the ones that have the most promise, and present them in such a way that readers will find them irresistible. Before we get on to the specifics of writing poetry, however, we need to take a brief look at the history of poetry to see why people write as they do today and how their methods differ from those of the past.

In a superb short essay on prosody, Galway Kinnell tells us that in the seventeenth century, rhyme and meter were meant to imitate a supernatural harmony, to "echo a celestial music." A poem like Milton's "At a Solemn Music" illustrates Kinnell's point:

> Blest pair of Sirens, pledges of heaven's joy,
> Sphere-born harmonious sisters, Voice and Verse,
> Wed your divine sounds, and mixed power employ
> Dead things with inbreathed sense able to pierce,
> And to our high-raised phantasy present
> That undisturbed song of pure concent,
> Ay sung before the sapphire-colored throne
> To him that sits thereon.

Here voice and verse, sound and sense, instrument and music combine to mimic the music of the spheres and send to heaven a pleasing if inferior copy of heavenly music.

In the eighteenth century, poetry became very worldly. Outward form was seen as a celebration of humanity's logical powers. Call it the Age of Reason, the Enlightenment, the Neoclassical Period—all of these names suggest that this is a period concerned with a mind that thinks rather than one that worships. God was still important, though increasingly distant; it was as though He had set the universe in motion long ago and then withdrawn, leaving humankind to scrutinize itself. Consequently there is an elegant, self-celebrating tone to much poetry of the eighteenth century, as in these lines from "A Little Learning" by Alexander Pope:

> Fired at first sight with what the Muse imparts,
> In fearless youth we tempt the heights of Arts;
> While from the bounded level of our mind
> Short views we take, nor see the lengths behind,
> But, more advanced, behold with strange surprise
> New distant scenes of endless science rise!

The Romantic and Victorian periods were marked by political and technological revolutions; they are really the beginning of what we call the modern era. Faith in both spiritual matters and human perfection began to crumble as the focus shifted from God (in Milton's day) to humankind (in Pope's) to the naked individual, helpless before changes he did not anticipate and could not comprehend. The confident "we" of "A Little Learning" becomes a questioning "I" in the poetry of Wordsworth, Coleridge, Shelley, Keats, and the poets who followed them. And as Kinnell says, rhyme and meter became charged with a new energy as they tried "to call back, in poetry, the grace disappearing from everything else."

Nowhere is this struggle for grace more evident than in the conclusion to Matthew Arnold's dramatic monologue "Dover Beach," with its irregular iambic pentameter line:

> Ah, love, let us be true
> To one another! for the world, which seems
> To lie before us like a land of dreams,
> So various, so beautiful, so new,
> Hath really neither joy, nor love, nor light,
> Nor certitude, nor peace, nor help for pain;

And we are here as on a darkling plain
Swept with confused alarms of struggle and flight,
Where ignorant armies clash by night.

Following World War I, it is the general consensus that the ignorant armies were victorious. Writers of the modern era can have no illusions about the disappearance of the world's grace, says Kinnell, which is why

for modern poets—for everyone after Yeats—rhyme and meter amount to little more than mechanical aids for writing.... In rhyme and meter one has to be concerned with how to say something, perhaps *anything*, which fulfills the formal requirements. It is hard to move into the open that way. If you were walking through the woods in winter, rhyming would be like following those footprints continually appearing ahead of you in the snow. Fixed form tends to bring you to a place where someone has been before. Naturally, in a poem, you wish to reach a new place. That requires pure wandering.

The following poem is a good example of a poet trying "to reach a new place."

Tropical Fish

Velvet sulphur powder puffs, and cream
And lavender arrangements trimmed with ice,
Little chandeliers and pulsing lanterns,
Lipstick streaks, and ermined eyes of gin
Shaken in cut glass, and sleighs of Roman
Stripes, and azure mirrors under skin,
Bones like silk embedded in a crystal,
Armor made of mica, gilded wine
Strung like buoys along a throbbing wire,
Snows collecting into white jade bulges,
Milktails of successive pale blue arches
Stippling into gray, G-clef signs
Descending slowly on their licorice threading—
Glass and waterglass, rain on rain.

HOWARD MOSS

The poet's primary tool here is diction; I get a very strong picture of Howard Moss chewing the tip of his pen, scowling at his fish tank, trying to come up with the precise combination of words to describe each species. Notice that there are some formal elements in this poem: for example, there are roughly five iambic feet per line, though the poet felt free to shorten or lengthen a given line as needed. There are some rhymes ("gin" and "skin"), but not enough to suggest that rhyming is of primary importance here. While Howard Moss is clearly tipping his hat to the formal tradition (he even uses the sonnet's standard fourteen lines), he is also taking a step away from it. The impression that the reader gets is not of a poet completing a task his predecessors have assigned him but a poet trying to break new ground and say something about his subject that has never been said before.

Later in the same essay, Galway Kinnell compares a poem to a journey, which should remind you of the earlier analogies in which A. R. Ammons likens a poem to a walk and Howard Nemerov likens it to a joke. Journey, walk, joke: you never know what will be waiting at the end. E. M. Forster once quoted an anonymous "old lady" who said, "How can I know what I think till I see what I say?" This sounds like T. S. Eliot's statement in his 1959 *Paris Review* interview: "One doesn't quite know what it is that one wants to get off the chest until one's got it off." Finally, Norman Mailer reminds us that "until you see what your ideas lead to, you know nothing." Only shallow people and charlatans begin with perfect knowledge of what it is that they mean to say. An honest writer begins in ignorance and writes his way toward the truth.

Only one thing remains to be considered, and that is how to bring the creative act to a fitting close. So much effort is given to starting and sustaining the creative effort that we sometimes forget about the difficulty and importance of ending on the right note. Getting the end of a poem right is one of the most exacting aspects of writing and one of the most important, for a hasty or ill-conceived conclusion may undo all the good work that preceded it. The poet Maxine Kumin once wrote an essay on this subject called, appropriately, "Closing the Door." At the end of every poem, says Kumin, there should be, "if not the slam of the door...then at least the click of the bolt in the jamb. My *bête noire* is the poem that ends by simply falling off the page in an accident of imbalance, so that the reader, poor fish, doesn't actually know the poem has ended. He turns the page in expectation of further enlightenment, only to be caught red-fingered with the title of the next poem coldly sizing him up." Instead of the clumsy non-ending, then, Kumin proposes four kinds of closure and gives examples of each, using both formal and free verse.

First is the poem that comes full circle. The last line of Frost's "Provide, Provide" echoes the title.

> Better to go down dignified
> With boughten friendship at your side
> Than none at all. Provide, provide!

There is also the poem that ends in an understatement that startles or arouses. Randall Jarrell's "The Death of the Ball Turret Gunner" is such a poem. A World War II aviator recounts his experiences in battle and then closes with these words:

> When I died they washed me out of the turret with a hose.

The tone is flat and unsensational. This flatness heightens the reader's horror as he realizes that the speaker is dead and that, in death, he is no longer a creature with soul and spirit; instead, he is a sanitation problem ("washed...out of the turret with a hose").

A third type of poem concludes with a prophetic or apocalyptic statement, as is the case with Yeats' "The Second Coming." Foreseeing the end of a historical cycle, the poet laments the passing of a better world and concludes questioningly:

> And what rough beast, its hour come round at last,
> Slouches towards Bethlehem to be born?

Finally, there is the poem that concludes with "an aggressive shift of balance" that totally reverses the meaning of the poem thus far. Such a poem is Edwin Arlington Robinson's "Richard Cory," in which the townspeople articulate their bitterness and their envy of the handsome, wealthy, supremely confident Cory, the man who embodies everything they want to be. Robinson's grip on the reader is so complete that no one, on reading the poem for the first time, can fail to be startled by the last lines.

> So on we worked, and waited for the light,
> And went without the meat, and cursed the bread;
> And Richard Cory, one calm summer night,
> Went home and put a bullet through his head.

Such endings are quite literally the last word in artifice. They complete the process of depersonalization that turns emotion into art, for unless the poet steps outside and closes the door, the poem remains a mere untidy slice of life—of personality, as it were.

Part Two
HOW TO WRITE POETRY

*The progress of any writer is marked by those
moments when he manages to outwit his own
inner police system.*

Ted Hughes

*What you have to realize when you write poetry,
or if you love poetry, is that poetry is just
naturally the greatest goddamn thing that ever
was in the whole universe.*

James Dickey

A Few Basic Rules

If you look over the poetry anthologies, the literary magazines, and the collections by individual poets of the last hundred years, you begin to detect, not a sameness, but an adherence to a few basic rules that seem to have served poets well over the decades. As you ponder these rules, you will immediately begin to think of exceptions—"well, E. E. Cummings didn't do it that way, and he's pretty famous!" Right. Cummings broke most of the rules and triumphed splendidly; just about everyone else who has broken these rules has failed. Too, Cummings achieved his poetic identity at least in part by his contempt for standards; you could do exactly what he did and become a ninth-rate version of E. E. Cummings, but wouldn't you rather become a first-rate version of yourself?

Just about every poet of any stature has begun by mastering the fashions of the day and then moving forward from there. Each of us wants to write the poetry of the future, but no one has ever broken new ground without first working within the poetic tradition. Don't worry about being influenced unduly by that tradition. If you are capable of developing a strong poetic voice, you will. The tradition won't harm you; in fact, it will give your poem a strength it would not acquire were it written in a vacuum. In his essay on "Tradition and the Individual Talent," T. S. Eliot tells us that when real poets emerge, they represent the poetic tradition, but in a new and forceful way, so that the poets of the past have to be re-read in terms of the genius who has altered them.

That should be the goal of each of us. First things first, however.

1. Write in sentences. Isolated images and poetic fragments will succeed occasionally, of course, but they will never pull together into a coherent whole. You will want all of your poem to affect your reader, not just a small part of it.

2. Use concrete language. Include details. Appeal to the five senses. In

"There Died a Myriad," his celebrated denunciation of the Europe that fought World War I, Ezra Pound doesn't refer to "a rotten bunch of countries" or "a bad place"; he makes his hatred real when he describes that corrupt culture as "an old bitch gone in the teeth." Remember, fiction is essentially narrative, and poetry is essentially metaphor.

On a test once, a student wrote, "Poetry is good for the poet—it is an outlet for his feelings," but then the student crossed out "feelings" and wrote "ideas" instead. The change made the student's sentence correct, because it is ideas that make us feel. "I hate the rich" is an idea that arouses emotions within us; so is "I want to live with you forever. Neither is a feeling *per se*. You will never be able to get your emotions down on paper, but you can say why you feel the way you do, and the result will be that the reader will have the same feelings that you do. This means using concrete language to tell me why the rich are so detestable or what it is about me that makes you want to be mine always.

3. Employ standard usage. A lot of new poets begin by combining words, coining new words of their own, and devising new spellings for the words we already have. The truth is that this is pretty easy to do, and while it might appear clever in one or two instances, it will never amount to poetry. (See Rule #1: "You will want all of your poem to affect your reader, not just a small part of it.") The real energy in a poem comes from fresh combinations of familiar words and ideas. Look out your window: is the "winterwind ablowing springward"? Big deal. Now look again: are the cows playing baseball? Congratulations. You have got the beginning of what could turn out to be a fine poem.

Don't use the lower-case "i" when referring to yourself; it looks like false modesty ("little ol' humble me"). Besides, so many people have done it before you that it has become a monumental cliché. Don't use too many ellipses...to show that you are in a dreamy mood . . . or you will begin to irritate the reader. . . . The same thing goes for exclamation marks! Either the excitement is there or it isn't, and you can't create it with punctuation! Watch out for archaic forms ("standeth," "o'er").

4. Write free verse, or at least avoid rhymes which force you to sacrifice ideas in favor of nursery-rhyme sounds. Of course, after you have developed your poetic voice, you can use rhyme to extend it in new directions, but the rhyme of beginning poets often sounds like bad

Joyce Kilmer. There is so much more to rhyme and meter than "I think that I shall never see / A poem lovely as a tree," and poets who get trapped within that tick-tock iambic line sometimes never escape.

Another point about rhyme: be careful not to confuse a song with a poem. One relies on music to complete it, whereas the other stands alone. Overeager critics sometimes call out greatest songwriters "poets," but it's usually the percussion that makes us want to get up and dance, not the lyrics. If you are a songwriter, the exercises you perform in a poetry class will sharpen your abilities as a lyricist, but when you try to write poems, write poems. The poem-as-song is liable to be an ungainly hybrid.

5. Title each poem effectively. Titles are more than mere conveniences; they add meaning to a poem. The idea that a title is necessary often brings out a great deal of resistance in young poets, but that is only because good titles are hard to come up with. Yet the struggle is worth it. If you have written a poem about an elephant who takes up residence in your backyard, an obvious title is "The Elephant." But isn't "The Elephant Who Came to Stay" more expressive? Or if you found out that the elephant came from outer space, then how about "The Elephant from Mars"? In a case like this, you can see how thinking about a title can get you to rethinking and possibly improving your poem. Emily Dickinson didn't put titles on any of her poems, but she wasn't planning on publishing them, either.

And remember, while any title is better than none, a good title will get the reader's attention; it might even make a mediocre poem seem better than it is. Besides, no one would be drawn to a poem called "Perspectives" or "My Vision," but who would not want to find out what's going on in a poem called "The Planet of the Dead Unicorns" or "The Movie at the End of the World"?

6. Type your poems. Statues are made of stone and clay, paintings are made of oils and watercolors, poems are made of print—not thought and feelings, but print. Print is the poet's medium, so get used to using it. Mastery of spacing, line length, and stanzas is essential; poetry is verbal, but it has a graphic dimension as well, and the way a poem looks determines how it is received. Editors have to see how poems look in print before they can even begin to think about accepting them, and while none of us has a printing press in the living room, with a little effort any of us can get access to a typewriter. Later in this book I will talk about submitting your poems for publi-

cation, but for the moment you should get used to the idea of working with print the way professional poets do.

In the first part of this book, you learned that a poem is like a walk. "A Step Away From Them" by Frank O'Hara is literally a stroll through the streets of New York, which are full of surprises. Read this poem and then consider it in terms of the rules you have just been given. In what ways does O'Hara appeal to your senses? How does the title focus or add meaning to what appears to be an incoherent list (who are the "them" of the title)? How do line length and stanza breaks reinforce the poem's argument?

A Step Away From Them

It's my lunch hour, so I go
for a walk among the hum-colored
cabs. First, down the sidewalk
where laborers feed their dirty
glistening torsos sandwiches
and Coca-Cola, with yellow helmets
on. They protect them from falling
bricks, I guess. Then onto the
avenue where skirts are flipping
above heels and blow up over
grates. The sun is hot, but the
cabs stir up the air. I look
at bargains in wristwatches. There
are cats playing in sawdust.
                              On
to Times Square, where the sign
blows smoke over my head, and higher
the waterfall pours lightly. A
Negro stands in a doorway with a
toothpick, langourously agitating.
A blonde chorus girl clicks: he
smiles and rubs his chin. Everything
suddenly honks: it is 12:40 of
a Thursday.
                Neon in daylight is a
great pleasure, as Edwin Denby would

write, as are light bulbs in daylight.
I stop for a cheeseburger at JULIET'S
CORNER. Giulietta Masina, wife of
Federico Fellini, *è bell' attrice.*
And chocolate malted. A lady in
foxes on such a day puts her poodle
in a cab.
          There are several Puerto
Ricans on the avenue today, which
makes it beautiful and warm. First
Bunny died, then John Latouche,
then Jackson Pollock. But is the
earth as full of life was full, of them?
And one has eaten and one walks,
past the magazines with nudes
and the posters for BULLFIGHT and
the Manhattan Storage Warehouse,
which they'll soon tear down. I
used to think they had the Armory
Show there.
          A glass of papaya juice
and back to work. My heart is in my
pocket, it is Poems by Pierre Reverdy.

               FRANK O'HARA

One of the most exciting discoveries that a poet can make is that anything is possible in a poem. Of course, a lot of hard work is necessary, and so is a lot of patience. Whatever you do, be sure you surprise yourself. Don't write what you already know. Give yourself lots of time—sit, stare at the wall, wait for ideas to come, take notes, assemble them when you have time, revise, revise again. And read, especially poetry in magazines, which is usually fresher and more daring than the poems that have been enshrined in anthologies. When you see that another poet has used an Italian phrase or written about bacteria or given his poem a diagonal margin, then suddenly you are free to do the same.

In the course of your reading, you will come across every type of poem under the sun. Because of their brevity, poems can assume forms that other genres cannot; after all, it is difficult to imagine an entire novel with a diagonal margin. People who say "I don't like poetry" might as well say "I don't like weather"; to treat poetry as though it is one thing only is just plain ignorant.

To impose a kind of order on the bristling, diverse species of poetry that populate today's literary landscape, I offer herewith six poems types. These are not only types of poems that are being written today, but they are types that are prominent in books and magazines (although, as the examples show, they are also types that poets have been writing for hundreds of years). More important than being prominent, they are also possible. After all, if somebody else can write these kinds of poems, then so can you.

Poem-Type One: Lists

The list is one of the oldest forms of poetry; it is also one of the most current. "The Song of Solomon" in the Judeo-Christian Bible is a timeless love poem in which the bridegroom lists the beauties of his adored bride:

> Thy navel is like a round goblet, which wanteth not liquor;
> Thy belly is like an heap of wheat set about with lilies.
> Thy two breasts are like two young roes that are twins.
> Thy neck is as a tower of ivory....
> And the roof of thy mouth like the best wine for my beloved,
>   that goeth down sweetly.

The Biblical bridegroom enumerates his beloved's body parts, praising as he goes. In one of my poems, which is also a poem about love, I make a list of the fantasy figures who sometime flood our minds when we get very excited.

In The Dark There Are Shapes Everywhere

> A man and a woman meet and fall in love
> and decide to go to bed together.

They undress, and he feels like a blacksmith
and she feels like a milkmaid

but when they begin to touch each other,
he feels like a bank teller working late

and she feels like a stuffy vice president
whose true beauty is revealed

once she takes off her glasses
and lets her hair down

and as he enters her,
he feels like a teenager in the back of Dad's car

and she feels like the new gym teacher
who has been warned about dating the students

but just can't help herself.
They begin to move faster,

and he feels like a renegade priest
and she feels like a nun

whose angry father and brothers
are about to burst in

and menace him with their knives
and pack her off to the country.

As they reach their climax,
he feels like a Knight of the Round Table

and she feels like a queen with a roving eye
and when it's all over,

he feels like an emissary wrongly entrusted
with somebody else's bride-to-be

and she feels like a king's fiancée
who has drunk a fatal love potion.

In the dark there are shapes everywhere,
eating our sleep.

DAVID KIRBY

You can see from these two examples that there is a natural affinity between feelings of love and the desire to make a list; when you love someone passionately, you want to go on and on about that person's charms or the things you want to do together or the places you will visit in your long and happy life.

There are forms of love other than the romantic variety, however. Christopher Smart's *Jubliate Agno* is a mid-eighteenth century testament to the poet's adoration of God. It is a curiously modern poem in its variety, its concerns with the ordinary, and its startling *non sequiturs*. In this passage, Smart is praising flowers as an example of God's handiwork. Notice that Smart is not concerned with the physical attributes of flowers but is instead thinking of all the particular ways in which flowers can be seen and understood.

For the flowers are great blessings.
For the Lord made a Nosegay in the meadow with his
    disciples and preached upon the lily.
For the angels of God took it out of his hand and carried it
    to the Height.
For a man cannot have publick spirit, who is void of private
    benevolence.
For there is no Height in which there are not flowers.
For flowers have great virtues for all the senses.
For the flower glorifies God and the root parries the
    adversary.
For the flowers have their angels even the words of God's
    Creation.
For the warp and woof of flowers are worked by perpetual
    moving spirits.
For flowers are good both for the living and the dead.
For there is a language of flowers.
For there is a sound reasoning upon all flowers.
For elegant phrases are nothing but flowers.
For flowers are peculiarly the poetry of Christ.

For flowers are medicinal.
For flowers are musical in ocular harmony.
For the right names of flowers are yet in heaven.
God make gardeners better nomenclators.

CHRISTOPHER SMART

Like any good poem, *Jubliate Agno* is full of surprises. And it is nothing if not all-inclusive: in this excerpt, Smart gives flowers abstract and even divine qualities ("For the flower glorifies God") as well as secular, practical ones ("For flowers are medicinal"). These delightful juxtapositions are refreshing, and they contrast forcefully with the blunt, repetitive beginning of each line.

The driving, cumulative effect of Smart's poetry gives it not only urgency but staying power, and it is no wonder that poets today still find this basic structure worthy of homage. Here is a poem contemporary poet Hunt Hawkins wrote about his cat.

My Cat Jack

For I will consider my Cat Jack.
For he is not like me.
For he wakes me in the morning.
For he proclaims himself with a yowl.
For when I stroke his head, he treadles my chest
    like a kitten getting milk.
For his mother is Kasha, his grandmother is Pippin,
    and his great-grandmother is Xanthippe, all living.
For he is Siamese.
For he cavorts under the sheets while I am making the bed.
For he stretches by kicking back his hind legs like a skier.
For he bows forward like a Mohammedan.
For he licks one paw clean, then tucks his head under that
    paw, and so the other.
For he sits on my desk and lays his ears down
    and appears to be an owl.
For he chases the balled up poems which I discard on the
    floor and so enjoys them despite their imperfections.

43

For he can move each ear by itself.
For from the side I can see through his eyes like water.
For he is easy in this life.
For he does not think ahead to death.
For he carries no cash.
For he does not have any pockets.
For he saves nothing, not even a bone.
For he eats what I give him, mainly Friskies.
For he is unemployed.
For even in the cat box he maintains his dignity
    and squats very straight.
For he does not know who the President is.
For he comforts my mind, which ceaselessly rolls in doubt
    and fear.
For in the asylum Christopher Smart loved his Cat Jeoffrey.
For in a rational century Rousseau doted on feline Ninette.
For in exile Vladimir Lenin had a cat for a friend.
For in fame T. S. Eliot respected all cats.
For young Jack is a small lion in my house.
For he looks out the windows for birds.
For he listens to the walls for mice.
For, despite everything,
    he is not maddened by domesticity.
For he leaps with real pleasure
    after a ribbon tied to a string.
For he inflates his tail.
For he fights with his back feet.
For in dry weather he is a bastion of electricity.
For he can find obscure heat.
For he curls about himself with his head upside-down.
For he sleeps.

HUNT HAWKINS

Of all the great list-makers in poetry, Walt Whitman is the one who gained the most advantage from this device, which, as the examples so far have shown, is basically simple yet capable of great variety and complexity. Whitman's critics refer to the "catalogs" (less sympathetic readers sometimes call them "laundry lists") which make up the bulk of his 1855 poem "Song of Myself." In the poems quoted thus far, the object under scrutiny has been the organizing principle of the list: a lover or a pair of lovers, flowers, a cat. Since Whitman's subject is the cosmos itself, no single object in it can suffice as the organizing principle. Whitman therefore uses himself as the spinal canal of the poem, and each of the objects he lists is a kind of vertebra; he wanders through the universe as a passionate yet detached observer, stringing together perception after perception until his poem is complete.

> The little one sleeps in its cradle,
> I lift the gauze and look a long time, and silently brush
>   away flies with my hand.
>
> The youngster and the red-faced girl turn aside up the
>   busy hill,
> I peeringly view them from the top.
>
> The suicide sprawls on the bloody floor of the bedroom,
> I witness the corpse with its dabbled hair, I note where the
>   pistol has fallen.
>
> The blab of the pave, tires of carts, sluff of boot-soles, talk
>   of the promenaders,
> The heavy omnibus, the driver with his interrogating
>   thumb, the clank of the shod horses on the granite floor,
> The snow-sleighs, clinking, shouted jokes, pelts of
>   snow-balls,
> The hurrahs for popular favorites, the fury of rous'd mobs,
> The flap of the curtain'd litter, a sick man inside borne to
>   the hospital,
> The meeting of enemies, the sudden oath, the blows
>   and fall....

Few of us are Whitmanian in our ambitions; after all, "Song of Myself" runs to about fifty pages. More typically, a list poem might try to catch the wonder of a particular setting that has strongly affected us at some point in our lives. Here is just such a poem by a student of mine. Like many a poem, it begins in the kind of childhood memory that comes and goes constantly in the mind of each of us, often when we are daydreaming or merely bored. As I explained in Part One of this book, boredom is a state which has occasioned an awful lot of poetry. A memory that means nothing to most people will be the beginning of a poem for others; David had probably thought of the old man and his treasure trove hundreds of times, but this time he made a poem out of his recollection.

The Life He Could Not Live

As I recall it now,
though I am old, and he
long since beneath the turf,
the old man's house was
a curious blend of times and styles.

As a child I went there
against parental whim
to see the things and hear
the tales and whatever else
could be got from him.

And there was much to be got
from him—there were green garnets
from Brazil gathering dust on a
homemade pine shelf, a bent pewter
hip flask on that same shelf,

smelling of recent use,
though, except for a certain twinkle
in his eye, the old man didn't
look like one to be calling
up the creature very often.

On the western wall an ebony
mask from dark Africa glared
through mirrored K-Mart sunglasses.
On an old gas heater by the door
a plaster skull, two rubber frogs,

a turtle shell, an old key and
some petrified wood vied for space.
On a table in the corner there was
a glass box full of foreign coins,
a stone head from Mexico, some

shark's teeth, arrowheads, rattlesnake
rattles and various bones from a
time too ancient for my young mind
to grasp. But the old man had a tale
for each, and for this I came back.

He had molas from Panama, souvenirs
from a war even my parents had forgot,
tapestries from Ecuador, palm bark dolls
made by real Indians in Florida, stone
money from Polynesia and a million

other odd and curious things
that one might pass by in a busy
life...a million odd and
curious memories that an old man
might share only with a child.

DAVID TRIMBLE

* * *

Exercises: An obvious kind of list poem is the poem to one's beloved; as Elizabeth Barrett Browning says, count the ways. The trick here is to throw in some seemingly inconsequential or even negative-sounding traits, bearing in mind that we often love people because of, rather than in spite of, their crooked teeth or tendency to roam around the house at night. List everything about something that is in the same room with you, such as a vase of flowers, and try to transform it into a new and startling world, as Howard Moss does in "Tropical Fish" on page 28. Paint a picture, as in the poems by Whitman and David Trimble; if nothing comes to mind, visit an art gallery (a great source of inspiration for all sorts of poems) or look at a photograph in a magazine like *Life*. Whatever you do, remember to "close the door"—list poems have a tendency to trail off, and you will need to do something decisive at the end.

47

Poem-Type Two: Marriages

This second type of poem I call a marriage; it contains two objects or ideas that are normally unrelated, and the poet's job is to unite them in a way that seems natural. I was tempted to call this type an argument after Yeat's assertion that we make poetry by quarreling with ourselves. But while it is true that most marriages have plenty of arguments in them, usually the arguments are resolved; otherwise, no marriage—and no poem. The trick is to treat two contrary themes or suppositions or whatchamacallits in such a way that the reader can never again think of one without automatically thinking of the other. If there doesn't seem to be any relation between your old baseball glove and Kant's *Critique of Pure Reason*, it's just because you haven't worked it out yet.

A student of mine who is something of a connoisseur wrote the following poem.

Sing a Song to Jenny Next

Tonight I'm uncorking a fine old wine,
my '78 Chateau Montelana cabernet sauvignon
that's been resting in my cellar for three years now.
I wanted to give it three more,
but that was before
I read Ricky Gardella's story.

Ricky Gardella, at age seventeen, as a U.S. Marine,
travelled a thousand miles through China
during the Korean war, blowing up an
atomic laboratory, killing a hundred or so Chinese
and one C.I.A. agent
so he could come home again.

No one expected him to survive.
Nobody wanted him to.
What he knew could have started a world war.
But he promised President Truman he wouldn't tell.
And he didn't, until twenty-five years later,

when he was dying of leukemia.

The government that sent him on his mission
did everything they could do to silence him,
keep him from publishing his story.
But his book came out in 1981,
the same year he died.

Tonight, my wine is my dinner.
I drink a choice vintage wine
solely to get drunk.
Tonight, I need to forget
that the seven years of this wine's age
may never be repeated.

CHARLES VIGNOS

What does someone's private wine collection have to do with a tale of
sabotage? Nothing—and everything. The story of Ricky Gardella,
which is purportedly true, is the history of someone who reached his
peak at a very early age and then spent the rest of his life almost as an
observer, a bystander witnessing his own decline. The speaker in the
poem came across Ricky Gardella's book in a casual or accidental
manner, it seems; the very tone of the poem suggests this. But most of
what we learn in life is acquired through happenstance, and from this
unpredictable encounter the speaker draws a powerful moral: we
often pay a heavy price for our greatness. For a brief moment Ricky
Gardella lived the kind of life that exists only in spy novels, and then
he entered into a long and painful decline, culminating in a harrowing
death. This is actually a fairly old story; it is the stuff of Greek
tragedy, in fact, with all its warnings against angering the gods.
Charles has made it fresh by introducing the business about the wine.
Wine has its proper term, and so does human life; between the
beginning and the end, many things can happen. The story of Ricky
Gardella reminds the speaker that a shining, glorious episode can be
the prelude to an absurd nightmare. In drinking the wine early and in
solitude, without companions or the accompaniment of a fine meal,
the speaker reenacts on another level the absurdity of Ricky Gardel-
la's life. If this sounds like a futile gesture, consider that by
performing what amounts to a sacrifice the speaker may be warding

off ill luck of his own. The ancient Greeks sacrificed what was precious to them for just the same reason, and if it did not prevent tragedy, at least their rituals provided them with some peace of mind.

If you feel daunted by the fact that you don't know enough about wine or the lives of spies, consider this next poem. All of us have cried. All of have been to the library. But it took Caroline Knox to put the crybaby in the library, with the following results.

The Crybaby at the Library

There was a crybaby at the library.
Tears were pouring heavily down his face.
He had omitted to do his math
and thought of the anger of his teacher
as the tears fell on his knitted
mittens between the fingers and thumb.

It is raining all over inside the library.
Parts of the brick walls are curling up
and plaster is falling on the heads and beards of students.
It is very dangerous for the books.
The rain comes down from every beam
and the professors do not know whether they should wrap
their articles in themselves or themselves in their articles.
The beautiful new botany professor who is only twenty-six
    and has marvelous dark eyes
has makeup running down her face as she runs out the door.

A precious incunabulum inside a glass case
is swimming gently as if in a dishpan.
Tiny letters and pieces of gold that were put there in 1426
are lifting off and turning into scum.
The assistant librarians are afraid to use the telephones
because yellow sparks are coming out of them.
Several young men go up to the attic, saying that the trouble
    may be from up there.
The electricity goes off and people are standing
between the floors in dangerously wet elevators.
The librarian's Kleenex and aspirin are wet and are melting
    into each other in the desk drawers.

The Shakespeare professors come out of the Shakespeare
    Room
and look around and go back in again; they must stay with
    the ship.
Fog is rising like rugs between the bookstacks.
People are laughing in a brittle way to disguise their well-
    grounded panic.

The botany professor is a redemptive figure.
She goes to the Maintenance Department and reports what
    is happening in the library.
Eventually the Maintenance Department goes over and fixes
    things.
The crybaby is definitely *not* a redemptive figure—he sits
still self-absorbed and shivery, and crying and crying,
and not at all trying to catch up on his math, nor even trying
    to fake it,
and all the time waves of water dash over his Bean boots
and up onto his lap, splashing his notebooks.
For the impending disgust of his teacher is foremost in his
    mind
as tears are foremost on his cheeks, where he sits crying and
    crying in the library.

CAROLINE KNOX

Somehow it seems natural for the little sniveller to slump there among the books, threatening everyone with drowning, and after a while, the poem becomes so horrific and goofy that we wouldn't want him to be anywhere else. Knox gives us here a fine example of the surrealism discussed in Part One of this book.

The next poem, which is by Emily Dickinson, brings together two things that appear to be even more unrelated than a crybaby and a library. Like all of Dickinson's poems, this one has no title, but because she was not writing for publication, she may be forgiven. (Those who do not plan to title their poems should be at least as great a poet as Dickinson is.)

David Kirby

A Route of Evanescence
With a revolving Wheel—
A Resonance of Emerald—
A Rush of Cochineal—
And every Blossom on the Bush
Adjusts its tumbled Head—
The mail from Tunis, probably,
An easy Morning's Ride—

EMILY DICKINSON

Dickinson forces us to be literary detectives: what's red and green (or emerald and cochineal) and flits from bush to bush? The ruby-throated hummingbird, of course. And the bird is also a high-speed train, its wings spinning like wheels as it delivers the mail which it picked up in the Middle East just that morning.

Dickinson is telling us that the sky is the limit, and maybe not even the sky. Here are two poems by students in which seemingly unrelated ideas or actions are married to each other in a tantalizing, resonant way.

Coconuts, Plane Crashes, and Mangos

While you were in New Jersey or Chicago growing up, ˄
Picking cherries or apples or something safe like that,
I was here, South Florida, picking mangos and
Coconuts, dangerous fruit.

The five of us, rich kids, too young to be purposeful,
Would toss mangos onto the golf course,
Or sit for hours pounding coconuts, Florida coconuts,
Against rocks to loosen the skins. Then we'd peel them off
Like animal hides
Until we had the insides ready to pitch
With vengeful ferocity onto the street.

We watched them crack open like we thought skulls might.

And when I heard about the plane crash,
About the death of two of the five,
I thought of the coconuts
And what life would have been like without them.

DAVID MORRIS

The speaker remembers when he and his friends split fruit open like cave people, enjoying the primitive ferocity of their wasteful behavior. When he learns that two of his old gang have died horribly, something in his mind connects their accident with his memories of boyish nonsense. Why is the fruit so important now? Because it was a way of bonding for the five friends, or a foreshadowing of the gory sundering of the group, or both? The speaker doesn't say, though he seems to be confident that we can draw our own conclusions.

In this next example, a classroom cut-up is given a well-deserved paddling, and the speaker thinks of a suicide.

Child Among the Crowd on Nassau Street
(At the Suicide of Tony Cartini)

Like in Old Lady Adams' Apple's class today:
Elwood Fritz stood up purposefully
and pissed in the trashcan.
(The old bag refused to give him a pass,
suspecting that he had already
"cried wolf" twice by that time.)
Perhaps he wanted merely to prove
that he wasn't really an Elwood Fritz.
Whatever the cause, we all knew
he was as good as dead.
She had a mammoth-sized weapon
with holes drilled in it for speed—
or at least for the sake of classroom propaganda.
"ONE—TWO—THREE—FOUR!"
Grinning, the rest of us chanted aloud
alongside the thunder of the Adams' Bomb,

David Kirby

as the object of doom came to be called,
finding ourselves a little less dead
through someone else's blows.

GLENN MARSH

The last two lines of the poem make clear the basis of this marriage: there is something about the violence suffered by others, whether it is self-administered or not, that firms up our own will to live. Notice there is only one reference to the suicide, and that is in the title, although the subtitle gives us a mental picture of a child standing outside a house where a friend or relative has killed himself and makes connections between that event and something that happened at school. If there is any reason to doubt the importance of titles, by the way, just try to imagine how this poem would read if it were called "P. S. 109" or "The Joys of Sadism." The poem would still work, but it would be much more limited.

This last poem is one in which I marry a story I had read about the composer Palestrina with something I saw one morning when I'd gone out for the paper. As I bent over, my hand outstretched, I happened to glance down the street and see two other bathrobe-clad men doing the same thing at about the same time. Nothing clicked until I read the anecdote about Palestrina, however.

The Dance of Husbands in Bathrobes

From the windows of the house
at the top of the hill
comes a stately music;
it is the funeral lament of Palestrina,
mourning his first wife
now that he is about
to take a second, a wealthy widow.

Men shuffle from doorways,
half-asleep; it is the Dance
of Husbands in Bathrobes.
They have something to say

54

with their slipper-shod feet,
their awkward hands,
unready for the day's work,
their thin, disorderly hair,
but they do not know what it is.

They advance, pick up the morning paper,
turn this way and that.
Wives and children rush to the window
to gasp and applaud
as the husbands leap higher and higher,
dancing and weeping—
the sun is breaking their hearts!
Look, look, they are sinking into
such sorrow as only happy men can know.

DAVID KIRBY

* * *

Exercise: Poetic marriages are a delight to perform. Anything goes as far as the subjects are concerned. Say you are driving along, thinking of your days at summer camp. You pass a field of cows and, as cows always seem to do, they turn in unison and watch you drive by. Camp. Cows. How about a camp for cows? After the boredom of the pastures, the cows would probably enjoy playing baseball and going to the archery range, and I can just see them around the campfire, telling bovine ghost stories. Or say you hear someone mention the name of Ulysses, surely a fit subject for a poem. Only don't write about Ulysses in Greece; Homer beat you to it a few centuries ago. Why not have him walking around the streets of New York, say, or San Francisco? Our epic hero might have adventures in those cities that would make the events of *The Odyssey* and *The Iliad* seem tame in comparison.

David Kirby

Poem-Type Three: Reversals

A reversal is a poem in which a stereotype or a received truth is simply turned on its head. For example, Dracula is always depicted as a loathsome bloodsucker in the novels, films, and ghost stories (bovine or not) that constitute our collective nightmare. I decided to give an unsuspecting world a Dracula who is charming and intelligent. The question was how. I thought of having an objective speaker describing the caped count as he moves through his domain, but a third-person account might not have the force I wanted. Dracula could deliver a dramatic monologue, of course, but then he might come off as arrogant and boastful. Then it occurred to me to show Dracula through the eyes of his bride; what could be more affecting, after all, than the love of a sympathetic woman? If someone ever asks Mrs. Dracula, "How did you meet your husband?" this is what I hope she would say.

Dracula's Bride

It was on the train
from Vienna to Budapest.
I had just left my husband.
You were reading Seneca
and I *The Imitation of Christ*.

There was a pear,
I remember,
and some cheese,
and when I cut my finger
you started from your seat.

How nervous we were!
A drop of moisture
hung from your lip,
and your eyes shone
in the gaslight
as you took the pins
from my hair.

That night
a wolf ran beside the train
for as long
as I watched.

DAVID KIRBY

No stakes through the heart here. Instead, the lovers are upper-class, well-read, and inclined toward gourmandise; that's a pear and some cheese they are sharing, not a meatball sub. And the whole scene is bathed in the gaslight of *la belle époque*. One of Dracula's children is running beside the train in the moonlight and the snow, but by now the conventional terror has been defused, and the energy that is usually frightful and life-threatening has now become sexual and affectionate instead.

In one of the great poems of the nineteenth century, Emily Dickinson performs a similar kind of reversal. The specter of death holds a certain horror for us all, which is why death is usually seen as an empty-eyed skull or the Grim Reaper or a shrouded figure that beckons us with a bony hand as the mist swirls, the dog howls mournfully, and the door to the tomb swings open with an agonizing creak. These images were boringly familiar even in Dickinson's day. Her portrait of death is fresh because it is favorable. Some readers say that death takes the form of a lover in the following poem, but probably the phrase "gentleman caller" would be a little more accurate.

Because I could not stop for Death—
He kindly stopped for me—
The Carriage held but just Ourselves—
And Immortality.

We slowly drove—He knew no haste
And I had put away
My labor and my leisure too,
For His Civility—

We passed the School, where Children strove
At Recess—in the Ring—

We passed the Fields of Gazing Grain—
We passed the Setting Sun—

Or rather—He passed Us—
The Dews drew quivering and chill—
For only Gossamer, my Gown—
My Tippet—only Tulle—

We paused before a House that seemed
A Swelling of the Ground—
The Roof was scarcely visible—
The Cornice—in the Ground—

Since then—'tis Centuries—and yet
Feels shorter than the Day
I first surmised the Horses' Heads
Were toward Eternity—

EMILY DICKINSON

The leaving of life is not without its unpleasant moments; the speaker seems reluctant to say goodbye to the things of the earth, and her mortal raiment offers little protection against the chill of the dew. But the good news is that there *is* life after death, and a fairly enjoyable life, too—after all, time is flying (" 'tis Centuries—and yet / Feels shorter than the Day"), and that doesn't happen unless we're having fun. Considering that this was a blind date, the speaker in the poem did well indeed.

In his novel *The Invisible Man*, H. G. Wells gives us a reprise of the Faust story; the moral is that if we acquire knowledge too powerful to control, we may bring about our own downfall. This basic allegory is always being updated, and if it is as old as the story of Adam and Eve, it is as new as the warnings against nuclear proliferation in today's paper. The story of irresistible temptation will always be compelling because we all want power, and none of us thinks he or she will be harmed by it. At least this is true for everyone except the Visible Man, an invention of mine and a reversal of Well's brave but flawed scientist. Consider the following poem and ask yourself if you know anyone like the main character in it.

The Visible Man

The police won't arrest this guy; he's the visible man.
Women don't scream when he takes off his clothes.
He doesn't have to keep to his room or talk to himself
like a lunatic. He is almost never seen writing
and experimenting with liquids. He does not arouse
the suspicions of many. No one takes him for a criminal
trying to avoid the grip of detection. No schoolteacher
postulates that he is an anarchist. He needn't escape.
He doesn't have to blunder into the house of Dr. Kemp,
an old school chum. Kemp doesn't have to
give him food and notify the police.
The visible man doesn't have to chase Kemp
and be overcome by a crowd and killed because he
was never half mad and bankrupt. He had no wish to start
a Reign of Terror. His story is a warning to us all.

DAVID KIRBY

As you read this poem, you may have sensed some of the enjoyment I got out of writing it. After a while, the reversals of the events in the life of Wells's character become absolutely ridiculous; can you imagine asking a friend what someone else is like, only to have your friend say, "Well, he is almost never seen writing and experimenting with liquids"? Yet I hope the ridiculousness takes on a certain significance after a while. For if the Adam/Faust/Invisible Man stories warn us against going too far, the Visible Man story is intended to warn us against not going far enough. Originally, the last few words of the poem were, "His story is a warning to no one." This is in keeping with the idea of reversal, of course—if Wells was warning us, I wanted to do the reverse. But by being so consistent, I ran the risk of writing a lesser poem. In the last half-line, then, I reversed the reversal. In the beginning and middle the poem extols a conservative lifestyle, but there is a twist at the end. Earlier in this book I comment on the necessity of an effective ending, and I hope I "closed the door" effectively here by suggesting that a person who never takes a chance will never be remembered.

In each of the examples offered thus far, a specific figure has been reversed: Dracula, death, the Invisible Man. This last poem portrays a world in which *everything* is reversed. Here I tried to turn the whole cosmos inside out and make all the normal processes go backward; there are a lot of special effects here, but as you will see, once all the fireworks stop, the result is a rather sedate love poem.

Sub Rosa

Maps would be literal if the normal order
were other than it is: letters would appear across
the faces of cities, and roads would become red lines.
Pages would fly out of books as well and then out of windows
to form trees in the yards of the literary.

The trees would shrink to seedlings and then seeds,
which would disappear up the anuses of birds
who would drop them where trees have never grown.
Gasoline would run out of cars and down hoses
into the earth, where it would turn into dinosaurs

who would escape through giant rents in the crust
to lurch down streets crowded with witches,
Manicheans, Confederate soldiers, Hunkpapa Sioux.
Everywhere things would extrude, exfoliate;
poems would be replaced by their meanings.

As for us, nothing would change.
For already when we lie down together or go for drives
or simply sit across the table from one another,
each look, each word, each touch bears out
the secret history of the world.

DAVID KIRBY

The point is a fairly simple one: no matter whether the world stays as it is or completely reverses itself, our love will always be the same, honey. Probably most poems begin simply; it's the working out of the complex details that provides the challenge—and the fun. I got a lot of enjoyment out of all the little reversals that make up this poem, and, needless to say, my wife was pleased to have a poem written for her.

Also, for weeks I had been looking for an excuse to refer to the Hunk-papa Sioux; I just liked the sound of their name. "Sub Rosa" gave me my chance.

* * *

Exercise: As I see it, reversals just make the world a more interesting place to live in. Why not charming werewolves, or mummies who need love (maybe that's why they stagger around with their arms out-stretched, making those awful sounds)? Many mysteries and much science fiction are reversals; the sweet old lady in the white gloves has just taken the vicar apart with her gardening shears, and as for that little house on the corner, well, for better or worse, it just happens to be located over the entrance to Hell. If you had bacon and eggs for breakfast this morning, why not have liver and onions tomorrow? By backing through your day, you'd be setting a good example for U. S. and Soviet leaders, who can only conceive of doing things one way, apparently; you might even bring about world peace by suppertime—excuse me, breakfast. Everything can be reversed. Take that cup of coffee you just finished: did you drink it, or did it drink you? I hope you didn't put the coffee to sleep. You have gotten a lot of good use out of that pen you're using, but I notice that it has a rather sinister cast as well; think of all the evil a pen is capable of. Get the idea? I hope so, since the hair is starting to grow into my head and crowd things in there. The worst of luck to you; may you back into some truly terrible poems!

Poem-Type Four: Forms

The older we grow personally, and the more "sophisticated" our society becomes, the more we have to wrestle with forms: tests, applications, licenses, notices, summonses, transcripts, receipts. Like the wily judo master, however, the poet will turn his culture's strength to his own advantage; a world that threatens to smother us with bureaucratic requirements can be made to topple under the weight of its own silliness.

One common form is the speech. We hear more speeches than we want to hear; I suppose that's part of the price we pay for living in a free society. If you ever feel as though you won't be able to take another line of political rhetoric, you might turn with relief to Allen Ginsberg's long poem "America," which is a speech addressed to the speechmakers.

America when will you be angelic?
When will you take off your clothes?
When will you look at yourself through the grave?
When will you be worthy of your million Trotskyites?
America why are your libraries full of tears?
America when will you send your eggs to India?
I'm sick of your insane demands.

. . . .

America you don't really want to go to war.
America it's them bad Russians.
Them Russians them Russians and them Chinamen. And them
          Russians.
The Russia wants to eat us alive. The Russia's power mad. She
          wants to take our cars from out our garages.

. . . .

America this is the impression I get from looking in the tele-
          vision set.
America is this correct?
I'd better get right down to the job.
It's true I don't want to join the Army or turn lathes in pre-
          cision parts factories, I'm nearsighted and psycho-
          pathic anyway.
America I'm putting my queer shoulder to the wheel.

                    ALLEN GINSBERG

Ginsberg's forerunner Walt Whitman used the speech form frequently; in a poem called "To a Common Prostitute" (quoted below in its entirety), Whitman addresses, not an entire nation, but one of its less reputable citizens.

To a Common Prostitute

Be composed—be at ease with me—I am Walt Whitman,
    liberal and lusty as Nature,
Not till the sun excludes you do I exclude you,
Not till the waters refuse to glisten for you and
    the leaves to rustle for you, do my words refuse
    to glisten and rustle for you.
My girl I appoint you with an appointment, and I charge
    you that you make preparation to be worthy to meet me,
And I charge you that you be patient and perfect till
    I come.

Till then I salute you with a significant look that
    you do not forget me.

WALT WHITMAN

The last line is a tip-off that the speech has taken place entirely in the speaker's head; poor Walt was too shy to actually say anything.

A form closely related to the speech is the letter; each is a form of address, the one spoken and the other written, to a person or persons. Or an insect, if you are Emily Dickinson.

Bee! I'm expecting you!
Was saying Yesterday
To Somebody you know
That you were due—

The Frogs got Home last Week—
Are Settled, and at work—
Birds, mostly back—
The Clover warm and thick—

You'll get my Letter by
The seventeenth; Reply
Or better, be with me—
Yours, Fly.

EMILY DICKINSON

I once wrote a letter-poem to the Argentine writer Jorge Luis Borges. (Notice that it is a type of reversal, too. There is nothing to keep these poem-types from crossbreeding with each other, after all.)

Letter to Borges

Dear Sir: you don't know me but that's not the point.
I have an idea which I think you can use.
It's not my idea anyway. Here it is:
last night my four-year-old son explained to me,
with perfect conviction, that the First Man and Woman
were actually named Wayne and Wanda
rather than Adam and Eve. Think of it, sir:
as the author of "Pierre Menard, Author of *Don Quixote*,"
in which you describe that friend of yours
who composed "not another *Don Quixote*—
which would be easy—but *the Don Quixote*,"
by which act of deliberate anachronism
and erroneous attribution he enriched
the hesitant and rudimentary art of reading,
surely you can imagine a world in which, for instance,
Napoleon might be named Waldo Davenport
and Caesar would turn out to be Bertram T. Watkins III.
And what if God Himself were named Bubba or Buddy?
When people prayed, instead of saying
"Almighty God, we implore thee,"
they would say "Hey, Bubba!" And other people would say
"His name's not Bubba, stupid, it's Buddy!"
and that would be one difference right there.
Of course you would want all the names to change
at one time, see: everyone would wake up
and all the famous people would have silly names
and vice versa. Think of the fun of it, sir! And the justice.

DAVID KIRBY

Another form common to poetry is the prayer. Gerard Manley Hopkins' "Pied Beauty" is a fine example.

Pied Beauty

Glory be to God for dappled things—
   For skies of couple-color as a brinded cow;
     For rose-moles all in stipple upon trout that swim;
Fresh-firecoal chestnut falls; finches' wings;
   Landscape plotted and pieced—fold, fallow, and plough;
     And all trades, their gear and tackle and trim.
All things counter, original, spare, strange;
   Whatever is fickle, freckled (who knows how?)
     With swift, slow; sweet, sour; adazzle, dim;
He fathers-forth whose beauty is past change:
               Praise him.

           GERARD MANLEY HOPKINS

The most irreverent scoffer can appreciate the beauty of Hopkins'
poem. By the same token, I hope that the most faithful of worshippers
will be able to see that although this next poem of mine has taken a
form that is secular in the extreme, nonetheless it too is a kind of
prayer.

How to Use This Body

Remove clothes and put to one side.
Body will look awkward, which is normal.
Arrange body on sheets, adjust temperature,
and turn out lights.

             At this point,
any number of things can go wrong:
phone can ring, vase or book can fall
from shelf, memory can quicken, love can beat
its wings against the window, and so on.
In that case read to body, give body

hot drink or bath, return body to bed,
and repeat steps two through four (above).

65

David Kirby

After several hours, remove body from bed
and wash.

Put body into clothes again.
Feed and love body. Do not cut, shoot,
hang, poison, or throw body from window.
Keep body from drafts and solitude.
Write us if you are happy with body, and
could we use your name in our next poem?

DAVID KIRBY

As the poem suggests, I am a light sleeper. People with this tendency often find that the body wants to be up and about just when the mind is thinking of nothing but a good snooze; the trick, then, is to cajole the frisky body into proper behavior. On one such sleepless night I must have been pondering the benign silliness of the world we live in, and what I came up with is a set of instructions of the kind that accompanies all those appliances and gadgets which, like our own bodies, have a tendency to malfunction. I tried deliberately to write that stiff, article-free language which characterizes such instructions, and then I hope I fell headlong into slumber, but I doubt it.

Not that it makes any difference: a bank teller or deep-sea diver with insomnia can only read or watch TV till the sun rises, but a poet who can't sleep should think of his wakefulness as a chance to get ahead of the competition.

* * *

Exercises: Give a speech. Tell somebody off. Write a letter to someone you love. Pray, and remember, you can pray to anyone or anything: your landlord, a movie star, a plate of fettucine Alfredo. Speaking of food, concoct a recipe. Conduct a survey. Write a review of your parents' childrearing practices or world history to date or your own poetry. Script a movie. Interview anyone on any subject; the more questions you ask, the more answers you are going to get, and if you get too many, you might even end up with two poems.

Poem-Type Five: Stories

While it is generally true that works of fiction tell stories while poems present images and impressions, there is also a venerable tradition of narrative poetry. Indeed, the first poems were probably stories; it was not until the rise of the novel in the nineteenth century that fiction began to reserve for itself the story-telling function. Still, the purpose of many a great poem is to do no more than tell a rattling good tale. Here are the first six lines of Robert Browning's " 'How They Brought the Good News from Ghent to Aix,' " probably written sometime in 1844:

I sprang to the stirrup, and Joris, and he;
I galloped, Dirck galloped, we galloped all three;
"Good speed! cried the watch, as the gate-bolts undrew;
"Speed!" echoed the wall to us galloping through;
Behind shut the postern, the lights sank to rest,
And into the midnight we galloped abreast.

Notice the speed at which Browning's speaker makes his getaway. He is in such a rush that he fails to introduce the third rider; our soldier-messenger is in such a rush to deliver news of the victory that it isn't until the second line that he mentions the name of his other companion.

A student of mine once wrote a story-telling poem that has an equally fast pace, but notice that the poem takes its speed not from physical action but from the rapid flow of the speaker's recollections. Hapless and besotted, the speaker's thoughts come to him in a rush, fueled by despair, a manic sense of humor, and not a little alcohol.

Hitchhiking in France

We're out on the road trying some hungover hitching
after getting drunk on Dover Beach last night
and ferrying across the channel to ride
the wrong train which left us at the station

David Kirby

in Lille where no one spoke English.
Oh, how I wish we had arrived in Amsterdam

instead. I'm mad at everything: at God, since Amsterdam
is far away; at Dominic, my scuzzy friend, for hitching
on to that nuisance of a girl with her haughty English
accent; and at her, too, for enjoying a border guard's offered
   night
of comfort while we sat stiffly in straight-backed station
chairs contemplating murder to get a quick ride

this morning. Why, God, does car after car ride
past? The sign that says it's a hundred kilometers to Amsterdam
might just as well be the graffito I saw in the Victoria Station's
john: "5,397 miles to Wall Drug, South Dakota." Hitching
is a helluva lot harder than those Yugoslavs let on the night
we ate and drank together in that distant English

pub. Now we're starved—having eaten only stale English
muffins saved from yesterday. We can't get a ride
and I feel abused, and as low as a hooked nightwalker.
I'm thirsty too, and dreaming of free beer in Amsterdam's
Heineken Brewery. So finally, fed up with hitching,
we consult our compass and head back towards the station

for tickets. At the first house we come to, I station
myself on the curb while Dominic repeats the English
word "rape" over and over to a confused woman hitching
clothes on a line. I guess the fool is figuring on a ride
from the French police. (We've heard that the cops in Amsterdam
let the red lights shine late into the night

and that they patrol the streets on horses, using nightsticks
for weapons.) I'm still staring into the gutter, my station
in life, beset by premonitions of arrest and brutality in Amsterdam
when Dominic convinces the woman through a French-English
phrase book to give us water. But we still can't get a ride
back to Lille, and I'm beginning to think it's impossible to hitch

in France. I just keep hoping that tonight we may hear English
again and have an Amsterdam goodtime. And later, as we ride

68

the right train out of the station, I pray for France's hitchhikers.

GEORGE ANDERSON

While a certain amount of dramatic tension is usually required, narrative poetry doesn't always have to rush at the reader with such breakneck speed. The following poem of mine is rather sedate, in fact. It was my intention that the poem have a fairy-tale quality and that the story unwind gradually, so that the characters would have time to contemplate the change in their lives.

The Bear

A bear came to our house one day in the spring.
He sniffed the seats of the chairs and put his head
in the refrigerator. We offered him pork chops
and hamburger patties, but he preferred cereal
and toaster waffles drenched with syrup.

We tried to interest him in an animal show on television,
but he wanted to watch a soap opera.
He sat with his paws in his lap and pretended not to cry,
but big tears rolled from his eyes
and dripped from the fur on his chin.

He stayed on into the evening,
and at cocktail time we poured him a saucer of gin,
which he lapped cautiously at first and then with gusto.
He liked our bed because the mattress was soft,
so we slept on the floor.

As the days went by,
he grew more philosophical and introspective
while we became more bearish, rolling about sluggishly
or snapping at the slightest provocation.
After several weeks we moved out altogether.

All summer long we have been catching fish with our bare hands
and raiding bee hives. Now the leaves are beginning to turn,

and we are getting our cave ready for the long sleep.
It will be our first winter, and we are apprehensive:
what if we don't wake in the spring?

Meanwhile, we shuffle down to the edge of the forest sometimes
and watch the bear go to work, dressed in my old clothes.
He has learned to drive,
though the car lurches and stalls a lot.
We have met some of his friends, and we like them very much,

though several of them resent us,
thinking we planned the whole thing ourselves.
Yet we would have gone on forever in the old ways
had the bear not taken our place.
We owe everything to the bear—that much is certain.

Often at night we talk about the bear
and wonder if he thinks about us at all,
if he moves down the days with nothing on his mind
or looks up at the door from time to time, as we did.
Now we know. Something always comes through.

DAVID KIRBY

Too, a poem which tells a story does not have to be nearly as long as the preceding examples suggest. Here is a very brief, pithy fable in poem form by Stephen Crane:

The Heart

In the desert
I saw a creature, naked, bestial,
Who, squatting upon the ground,
Held his heart in his hands,
And ate of it.

I said, "Is it good, friend?"
"It is bitter—bitter," he answered;
"But I like it

Because it is bitter,
And because it is my heart."

STEPHEN CRANE

One more example. Like the others, this poem is primarily a story, but as the title and the first three words suggest, it is also a letter, as in Poem-Type Four, "Forms." Again, there is nothing to keep a poem from having the characteristics of several different poem-types at once, and you might find it useful to look for the different elements of the different types in poems you encounter in other books and in magazines.

To My Sons

Boys, forgive me: if I'm ill-tempered in the morning,
it's because I spend my nights saving you from men
far worse than the monsters in your books.
You wouldn't believe these jaspers.
Why, once they took you to Mexico
and kept you awake for a week
and made you sit in straightback chairs
in a room where rattlesnakes slithered on the floor.
You fellows should have seen your dad:
just as you were falling off the chairs,
I kicked the door in and scooped you up.
With a boy under each arm, I stamped the snakes
to death and laid out the guards with spin kicks
to the groin and temple. We ran like hell
for the jeep and the survivors opened fire,
but we got out of there thanks to some fancy wheel work,
and now that we're home again with your mother,
I just want to say that I hope you boys
were paying attention back there in Mexico,
because you might be fathers yourselves some day
and believe me, those men will still be there.

DAVID KIRBY

* * *

Exercises: Some stories have already been written for you before you even think about putting them in poem form. For example, search through your childhood memories. Any memory that is recurrent is one that is significant enough to be expanded into a story poem. You can also get a story started just by creating an improbable situation; once you let the bear into the kitchen, the story will more or less write itself. Non-fiction prose is a great source for stories, especially if you have the discipline to put the book down and finish the story yourself rather than find out how the author ended it. (I did this once with the story of a kidnapper; when I went back and finished the book, I was glad to see that it ended differently than my poem did—and much less interestingly, I would like to think.) Remember that narrative poetry is your one chance to get some good out of the disgraceful episodes in your life. I am sorry you had to go to jail that time, and I really do believe the police should be more understanding about these things, but at least you can get a poem out of it.

Poem-Type Six: Schemes

In the first part of this book, I discussed the evolution of poetic form from roughly the seventeenth century to the present, showing how formal verse became free verse—not without a struggle, to be sure, yet in a way that, with the hindsight the years have given us, seems logical and natural. In the five poem-types considered thus far, rhyme and meter, the elements of traditional prosody, have been less important than the arrangement of lines upon the page. In most of the examples we have looked at, stanza length, line length, line breaks, and punctuation have been the poets' primary tools.

This is not to say that poetry without rhyme and meter is not rhythmical or that it is merely cut-up prose, as some of the die-hard enemies of free verse claim. The poet Philip Levine writes a very sensual-sounding free verse; an interviewer once asked him about his characteristic poetic line, and Levine replied that he was deliberately imitating Yeats' basic trimeter, which Yeats would use in

a song-like way or mold...into long paragraphs of terrific rhythmic power. I was very early awed by the way he could keep the form and let the syntax fall across it in constantly varying ways, the way certain sixteenth-century poets could with pentameter. The short line appeals to me because I think it's easier to make long statements that actually accumulate great power in short lines. You can flow line after line, and the breaks become less significant because there are so many of them, and they build to great power.

The following poem by Levine illustrates his method. As you can see, there is more craft in the writing of this free-verse poet than there is in the poetry of some third-rate sonneteer who is merely pouring words into a mold.

The Doctor of Starlight

"Show me the place," he said.
I removed my shirt and pointed
to a tiny star above my heart.
He leaned and listened. I could feel
his breath falling lightly, flattening
the hairs on my chest. He turned
me around, and his hands gently
plied my shoulder blades and then rose
to knead the twin columns forming
my neck. "You are an athlete?"
"No," I said, "I'm a working man."
"And you make?" he said. "I make
the glare for lightbulbs." "Yes,
where would we be without them?"
"In the dark." I heard the starched
dress of the nurse behind me,
and then together they helped me
lie face up on his table, where blind
and helpless I thought of all
the men and women who had surrendered
and how little good it had done them.
The nurse took my right wrist
in both of her strong hands, and I
saw the doctor lean toward me,
a tiny chrome knife glinting in

73

one hand and tweezers in the other.
I could feel nothing, and then he said
proudly, "I have it!" and held up
the perfect little blue star, no
longer me and now bloodless. "And do
you know what we have under it?"
"No," I said. "Another perfect star."
I closed my eyes, but the lights
still swam before me in a sea
of golden fire. "What does it mean?"
"Mean?" he said, dabbing the place
with something cool and liquid,
and all the lights were blinking on
and off, or perhaps my eyes were
opening and closing. "Mean?" he said,
"It could mean this is who you are."

PHILIP LEVINE

And now for a surprise. After all that has been said in favor of free verse and against traditional prosody, I would like to end with several poems based on schemes or strict verse forms. I may have slipped one by you already; if you thought George Anderson's "Hitchhiking in France" had a somewhat repetitive sound to it, you were right, although the repetition, far from being accidental, is due to the fact that the poem is a sestina. The sestina is a verse form which originated in the middle ages in the Provence region of France. There are six unrhymed stanzas, and the last word of each line in the first stanza is repeated in a fixed order in the succeeding stanzas; the poem concludes with a tercet (a three-line stanza) in which the six key words are used two to a line. It sounds complicated, but the sestina is great fun to write, because once you have finished your first stanza, then all you have to do is put down the key words (following the order George uses) in the right-hand margin and write lines to suit.

A similar poetic scheme is the villanelle, which is also French in origin. The villanelle consists of five tercets and a quatrain, and there are only two rhymes used. Because of the limited rhyme scheme, the villanelle is usually thought of as being restricted to light verse or poems that profit from a kind of church-bell rhythm, such as a poem in celebration of a marriage. In the following example, however, the poet has deliberately used the sounds of the villanelle to suggest the way we wake up, that is, by alternating between sleep and wakefulness until we finally realize who and where we are and that yes, it is time to face the world.

You Dream You Are Stationary

You dream you are stationary. Like books,
your eyes are shut. Asleep, you fear you're dead.
You move to open your eyes, take a look.

The Antarctic, you've read, is white, is stark.
Like your bed. You pull the sheet over your head.
You dream you are stationary, like a book,

like snow like white sand, unlike the dark.
You are hot. Morning breaks. Light hits your head.
You move to open your eyes, take a look.

The Sahara, you've read, is light, is blank.
Like your head. The sunlight's passed over your bed.
You dream you are stationary, like a book,

like white sand like snow, like the dark.
You are cold. You pull the sheet from over your head.
You move to open your eyes, take a look.

Like sheets of blank paper, your sheets are blank.
You fear nothing. You sink deep, as if dead.
You dream you are stationary, like a book.
You move to open your eyes, take a look.

SANDRA SPRAYBERRY

The villanelle can be written the way the sestina is written, that is, by setting up the key words first and then filling in the rest of the lines.

In both of these examples, the schemes the poets are using are very old, but the poems themselves are very fresh and contemporary-sounding; it is impossible to imagine either "Hitchhikers in France" or "You Dream You Are Stationary" being written at any time other than in the last quarter of the twentieth century. The point is not to study the schemes used by the poets of the past and then ape them uncritically. Rather, the idea is to give the old schemes new life by putting them to contemporary uses.

The following poem is clearly an homage to the traditional fourteen-line sonnet, as was Howard Moss's "Tropical Fish" on page 28, though without the strict rhyme and meter (there is an identifiable iambic foot, but it is used very loosely, and there are between four and six feet per line, as opposed to the strict pentameter of the conventional sonnet). Too, the subject is a little bit different from what the love poets of the Elizabethan and Jacobean era had in mind.

When Robots Make Perfect Love

Ah, if I could and they would but understand,
I would warn them of the danger: how like salmon
flashing over falls their metal bodies seem
in the sun, how like lemmings swimming
through lakes to gain the sea they are
in their desire, how we humans, confounded
by their neglect, have discovered their secret tryst
and watch from afar like jealous, silly gods.
But my words would mean nothing. Beyond
programming, beyond what they are or were meant
to be, beyond all they have been, they consummate
their passionless love without memory or guilt:
like the first lovers whose names they bear, they
embrace like statues, awaiting our covetous judgment.

GEORGE ANDERSON

Besides the robots, something else that strikes me as very modern about this sonnet is the use of that word "covetous" in the last line (which is hinted at by the reference to "jealous, silly" humans six lines earlier). Most of us would expect the speaker to slight these mechanical marvels and exalt humanity, but it turns out that the humans in this poem envy the robots and their technological love, which is untouched by mortal heartache and disappointment. This is a good example of how the meaning of a poem may turn on a single word.

This next poem is neither sestina nor villanelle nor sonnet nor any other traditional form, though its scheme is very regular: three five-line stanzas with an AABBA rhyme.

As a Child in Dayton

The snowplow left the narrow street tonight
with a wall on the left and a wall on the right,
and in the midst, the trail they always seem to miss.
I feel the snow flurry's gentle kiss,
walking late on the wintry white.

The sounds of the Fifth Street Church bell
confuse the chatter where some people dwell,
as do my steps, the crunches of snow I hear
being that much more to slowly disappear,
then lose into the wayward northern gale.

The glowing window lights from warmer places
make vague silhouettes of the unknown faces.
But I've my own, into the year's darkest night,
while treading upon the virgin crust of white
with little thought to any further spaces.

GLENN MARSH

So many rhyming poems by novices use a four-line AABB or ABAB scheme, but Glenn keeps the reader pleasantly off-balance with his variation on the traditional form; when you come across that unexpected fifth line, it's like getting an extra scoop of ice cream or finding another present under the Christmas tree. Glenn also varies the sound of his poem by using slant rhyme or near rhyme (thus "gale" rhymes, or almost rhymes, with "bell" and "dwell"); if you go back and look at the Emily Dickinson poems in this book you will see that slant rhyme is one of her most effective devices. Too, Glenn uses run-on rhyme or *enjambement*, in which a line continues into the next line without punctuation, as in the first two lines of each stanza. Since there is no period or comma to stop you at the end of "tonight," "bell," and "places," the rhyming words "right," "dwell," and "faces" strike your ear softly rather than harshly. Run-on rhyme is one of the best ways to avoid the tick-tock, nursery-rhyme sound of so much formal verse.

From time to time I encounter a formal poem so exquisite that it is impossible to imagine a free-verse "translation." Such a poem is Janet Burroway's "Nuns at Birth"; to tamper with the form would be to destroy the beauty. Notice again how slant rhyme and run-on rhyme are used to vary sound and pace.

Nuns at Birth

This wing is quick with nuns. They flock and flutter,
Their habits whisper, sweeping the corridor.
The mildest human sound can make them scatter
With a sound like seed spilled on the immaculate floor.

They know about waste. They come with disinfectant,
Troubling the peonies bursting on my sill;
Their quick white hands can purge the most reluctant
Stain, and the sprouting germ, and the alien smell.

Old men have said—and my anxious, Baptist mother—
That purity is the fallow ground of love.
It is here in the sterile sheets and the smell of ether,
And their bead-bright eyes. But what are they thinking of?

Or that Mother Superior about her labours:
What discipline could inform so bland a nod
When I shrieked and he shrieked and the bursting fibers
Gave him up to her quick white hands in blood?

Or the dove-grey novice now in her sterile plumage,
Who will go about birth, and about it: his hot greed
And my thickly weeping breast—what sort of *homage*
Brings her white hand fluttering to that bead,

Because it is that, my love! Her breath has quickened
At the noise of his pleasure in the immaculate air

As if some glory sanctifies the fecund!
Well. Twenty centuries' lies are brought to bear

In her innocent misconception; the germ sprouting
In the cell, the chalk on the alien door, the hot
Salvation of witches, the profits and the prating—
We have not bought those lies. But we must have bought

Some lies. We are consumers, you and I.
And now this third, gums leech-fast at my breast,
Whom we shall wean to an epicure, and say:
Self-sacrifice is ingratitude, is waste;

And say: husk the kernel; feed at the fountains;
Seek sun in winter at the belly of the earth;
Go to the east for splendour, the north for mountains;
And always go to the nuns in time of birth.

JANET BURROWAY

♥ ♥ ♥

Exercises: I suggest you start with a villanelle and then try a sestina. These highly artificial forms will get you used to the requirements of formal verse while helping you to avoid the easy rhymes and sing-song rhythms that less demanding forms allow. After that, try a "loose sonnet" of the type written by Howard Moss and George Anderson, or invent a form of your own, remembering to avoid nursery-rhyme sounds through *enjambement*, slant rhyme, and rhythmical variations. If you end up sounding like Mother Goose anyway, desist immediately. Some people were never meant to write formal verse, just as some people were never meant to write anything else.

David Kirby

A Final Word

As the preceding section suggests, formal schemes are alive and well and are still part of the poetic tradition. The difference is that, instead of dominating the tradition, formal verse is now only a part of it, and an increasingly smaller part at that. The poets whose formal verse I have quoted are still primarily free-verse poets. Too, most of them began with free verse and tried formal poetry only after they felt comfortable with the individual poetic voices they had developed through study and practice.

Each of us has such a voice already, a combination of syntax, diction, and subject matter that is identifiably ours. However, the reason why each of us is not a Nobel Prize winner is that, in our generosity, we share this voice with millions of others. If you listen to the babble in a shopping mall or sports stadium you soon realize that you are hearing, not hundreds of different voices, but five or six voices with some slight variations here and there. On the other hand, there is no mistaking the voice of Winston Churchill or W. C. Fields or Elmer Fudd. By the same token, the voices of Gerard Manley Hopkins and Emily Dickinson and Philip Levine are theirs alone. They sound like no other poets, and no other poets sound like them, except very remotely.

A beginning poet will sound like most other speakers in general. A poet who has developed through training and practice will often sound like other poets of the day, the twenty or thirty who dominate magazine verse and book publication and who will be largely forgotten in a few years. And once every generation or so, there will be a poet who, through talent and perseverance and sheer good luck, is able to develop a voice so powerful and mesmerizing that, like the Wedding-Guest listening to Coleridge's Ancient Mariner, we "cannot choose but hear."

Appendix A

GETTING UNSTUCK

No one should feel as though he or she has to write a poem every day or every week or even every month. But the time will arrive inevitably when you have not written anything for a while and you want to, yet you don't really have any ideas concerning where to begin.

First, don't neglect the obvious. Look again through the first part of this book and remind yourself of how many poems begin: in patient waiting, meditation, even boredom. Time and silence are a poet's most valuable resources. We live in a howling blizzard of electronic signals, industrial noise, other people's voices. So find a quiet place. Be patient yet vigilant. Let the poem come to you; inevitably, it will.

Another method is more or less the opposite of the above. This is to go out and get a brand-new legal pad and pen and start writing. Fill page after page with whatever comes to mind. You are likely to begin with surface description and immediate occurrences, but soon your conscious mind will tire and the unconscious will begin throwing ideas and images to the surface: memories, odd associations, revelations, feelings you never knew you had. Sooner or later, something will come to mind that can be made into a poem.

A third method and one from which I have benefited immensely is so evident that many poets overlook it. This is the method of research. All non-fiction writers have to do research, and if a novelist is going to plot a chase through the streets of Rome or reveal the intensity of an open-heart operation, he is going to have to spend some time in the library. Why not the poet, then? There is an image of the poet drinking absinthe or smoking opium or having a breakdown that runs counter to the mental picture we might get of the same person trotting happily up the library steps, hair neatly combed, newly-sharpened pencils in hand. But if you don't have an addictive personality anyway and if you suffer from nothing worse than the mild neuroses that the rest of us have, you should consider research as a means of coming up with poetic ideas. After all, if the poem is good, it doesn't matter if it was conceived in the library or at a black mass.

There are two ways you can use someone else's writing to further your own. The first I will call "weak research." Weak research simply means looking at other people's poems until you get an idea for one of your own. For example, when I had the itch to write once but couldn't find a subject I liked, I went out and found a poem in a magazine called "The Camel" by Nicholas Rinaldi, a poet I had not heard of at that time. In the poem a camel appears in the middle of a busy highway, and all sorts of miraculous things ensue. I decided to write "The Bear," which is included in this book. My poem is quite different from Nicholas Rinaldi's, but it never would have been written if I had not seen his first.

You can also do "strong research," which is the kind of formal research you might do for an article or term paper, complete with card-catalog searches, note-taking, the preparation of outlines, and so on. The following poem is one I wrote out of admiration for Sigmund Freud, a rarity among intellectual pioneers in that he not only founded a science but brought it to maturity in his lifetime. Freudian psychoanalysis has its flaws and shortcomings, to be sure, but the more I learned about it, the more I appreciated its essential practicality. Above all, I sensed behind Freud's writings a quality that others have overlooked, namely, the quality of compassion. Like the image of the poet, the image of the psychoanalyst is often distorted. Indeed, it is often deliberately distorted, and while so many would-be saviors decry the sterility of psychoanalysis and offer instead their own brand of instant transcendence, Freud began his long journey with the intent of helping the emotionally paralyzed citizens of Vienna he saw every day and ended by giving them the gift of the ordinary world—not the false heaven of some guru but the world of bills and backaches, a world of little pains and pleasures instead of the hell of their own emotions. But since I didn't know as much about actual Freudian practice as I needed to know, I had to read some of Freud's writings, the standard biography, and several articles about psychoanalysis. The following poem is the product of that research. It is therefore somewhat more factual than we generally expect a poem to be. Perhaps for that reason I use the tag "to take the young men only" early in the poem and repeat it in a gently self-mocking way. After all, few good poems are without their elements of irony and self-doubt; too, what Freud said is often more applicable to men than to women.

Saving the Young Men of Vienna

How bad it was, how embarrassing, to have been a young man
(to take the young men only) in Freud's Vienna, to go
to prostitutes and get syphillis and gonorrhea
or masturbate and become neurasthenic and then impotent,
to marry and either give new wives these terrible diseases
or dangle before them helplessly, driving them mad.

And even if these young men (again, to take the young men only)
were to make their way through the snares and pitfalls
of sexual development without accident,
avoiding the scarring experiences that turn young men
into fetishists and inverts, still they would sink
to the pavement of Vienna, finally, in sheer Oedipal exhaustion.

Therefore, how wonderful it was, how truly wonderful,
for the great Dr. Freud, not just an enormous intellect
but a genius, in fact, though a profoundly disturbed man
in his own right, one so shy that he had to sit
behind these troubled fellows so that he would not have
to be stared at all day long, to listen to their recitations

without directing his attention to anything in particular,
maintaining the same "evenly suspended attention"
in the face of all that he heard, allowing the patient
to drift without aim, without desire,
only interceding to help repetition become remembrance
as the patient surrendered his hysterical misery

and rose, pale and shaken but more certain
than ever before in his life, to go again
into the streets of Vienna and stroll about freely,
greeting old friends, pausing to buy a newspaper
or smoke a cigarette, doing precisely as he pleased,
embracing at last the common unhappiness.

DAVID KIRBY

The next poem is the result of research as well. It is about John Ruskin and his celebrated marital mismatch. Here the facts pretty much stand for themselves; the twists and turns of Ruskin's unhappy life are interesting in their own right and there is no need for the same kind of exposition of ideas that characterized "Saving the Young Men of Vienna." Still, this a poem, not history. The events of the last four stanzas occur out of sequence, so if you really want to know about Ruskin's final days, you should read his biography and his letters, as I did. Art is a shaped version of life; learning history from a poem is like thinking you understand the American Civil War after watching *Gone With the Wind*.

Patience

His first marriage annulled due to chronic impotence
(though he could masturbate, he said, telling his friends
he had become another Rousseau), he puts it aside forever:

the loneliness, the desire to have someone to come home to,
to take tea with, someone to *see*, then the meeting with Effie Gray,
the courtship and engagement, the long ride after the ceremony,

she with her period, he with a bad cold. Worse, there was the hair:
Ruskin had seen it in pictures of naked bawds, but a wife
should be as white and smooth as a statue, he thinks.

They put off consummation, agree to it, put it off again,
associating the act with babies, whom Ruskin finds too small,
until Effie ends the marriage, later entering into

a conventionally happy union with the painter John Everett Millais
as Ruskin finds his head turned increasingly
by the thirteen-year-old Irish girl Rose La Touche,

whom he is to court by letter.
Getting no satisfactory reply, he seeks messages
from her through random openings of the Bible,

dreams of her, sees her name hidden within other names, carries
with him one of her own poor letters between thin sheets of gold
and offers it to her at a chance meeting in the Royal Academy.

Rose, now anorectic and soon to die, says "no" as he offers
the gold-wrapped letter, "no, Mr. Ruskin," again and again.
Seven years later he finds that he cannot stop thinking of her.

One night he flees Oxford for an inn in Abingdon
where he leaves the door open and, on returning,
sees that the wind has blown the melting candle wax

into the shape of the letter "R."
Beginning a new cycle of hope and despair,
he journeys to Venice, where he takes as gondolier

a horrid monster with inflamed eyes as red as coals
and, setting out for the Convent of the Armenians,
becomes lost in the fog, landing at the madhouse on the island

of San Clemente. There he waits for something, anything,
a voice from the outside. Suddenly there are fireflies!
The black water seems measureless as they flicker and reappear.

DAVID KIRBY

Appendix B
GETTING PUBLISHED

First, don't be in too big of a hurry. Learn your craft well, and
publication will take care of itself.

There are lots of arguments against sending out your work too
soon. A young, skillful writer might be encouraged by early
publication to simply imitate himself and never grow. An immature
writer but one capable of real growth might be discouraged by early
rejection and never go anywhere. Finally, poor writers just clog the
system with their work and ruin the sight of editors who are then too

bleary-eyed to recognize work of real merit. The poet Robert Bly cautions waiting until at least age thirty-five to send out work; this is a little extreme, but it is certainly better than sending out your first handwritten efforts, as some people do.

Second, have a chat with your local poet. Most experienced writers are happy to talk to novices, either to fan the spark of talent or suggest that the hopeless case end his or her frustration and pursue some other interest. I may not know what makes a work a masterpiece, but I can tell you fairly quickly whether or not your poems are the kind that editors are publishing in magazines today.

Third, go to the library. You should be reading poetry constantly just to see what you can learn from other poets, and as you do so, you see what magazines accept what kind of poems.

Unfortunately, few libraries have as comprehensive a selection of literary magazines as they might have. Most, however, have the following indispensable guide, which you can also order from the address given below:

> *The International Directory of Little Magazines and Small Presses*
> Dustbooks
> Post Office Box 100
> Paradise, California 95969

The *Directory* contains literally thousands of detailed descriptions of magazines the world over, though mainly in the U. S., England, and Canada—what they publish, how much they pay (if anything), how long it takes them to reply.

Two periodicals every writer should subscribe to are:

> *The AWP Newsletter*
> Associated Writing Programs
> Old Dominion University
> Norfolk, Virginia 23508-8510

> *Coda: Poets & Writers Newsletter*
> Poets & Writers, Inc.
> 201 West 54 Street
> New York, N. Y. 10019

Each issue of these two newsletters contains not only informative articles about the publishing world but also solicitations from magazines who are currently reading manuscripts, reminders about grant applications, and so on.

A journal featuring detailed reviews of literary magazines plus an annual survey of new magazines (that is, ones which might be particularly hospitable to new writers) is:

Literary Magazine Review
Department of English
Kansas State University
Manhattan, Kansas 66506

* * *

Here are some guidelines that will help you with the often frustrating yet ultimately rewarding business of poetry submission.

1. Never submit blindly. Try to examine several back issues of the publication to gain a sense of what the editor wants. It isn't reasonable, for instance, to expect a newspaper to take the space to print an epic poem.
2. Submit four to eight poems at a time—enough to give the editor a choice, but not enough to give him or her a headache.
3. Everything should be typed—name, address, envelopes, poems.
4. Be sure the ribbon on your typewriter is reasonably new. Light type is too difficult to read, especially in quantity, submission after submission.
5. Set each poem on the page with the lining and spacing exactly as you would like it to appear in print.
6. Submit no more than one poem per sheet of paper.
7. Don't send your one and only copy of a poem.
8. Paper should be full-size white typing paper, 8½" x 11".
9. Always include a self-addressed envelope with adequate postage. If sending to magazines in other countries, be sure to enclose International Reply Coupons instead of stamps.
10. Use the right size envelope. Too small a one crushes your work. Too large a one, and the post office will bend it.
11. Your name and address should be on both envelopes, on each poem, and on any other enclosures.
12. Include a short covering letter or biographical sketch if you wish, recounting a bit of your personal history and some of

your publishing credits. But don't tell the editor why your poems should be published; the work will stand or fall on its own merits.

13. Give the editor around three months to reply before inquiring.
14. If the publication sees daylight complete with your poem, international ethical standards dictate that you should receive a free copy; if you are lucky, there may be a small check as well.

And remember—editors don't reject; they merely select.

Appendix C
FURTHER READING

Three indispensable guides to poetry and to literature in general are Karl Beckson and Arthur Ganz, *Literary Terms: A Dictionary*, revised edition (New York: Farrar, Straus and Giroux, 1975); Babette Deutsch, *Poetry Handbook: A Dictionary of Terms*, 4th edition (New York: Barnes and Noble, 1982); and C. Hugh Holman, *A Handbook to Literature*, 4th edition (Indianapolis: Bobbs-Merrill, 1980). All of these are published in paperback and should be in the library of every writer and book lover.

The following books are all referred to in the preceding text. The acknowledgments page at the front of this book lists the poets to whom I am indebted, and here I should like to tip my hat to the literary critics, biographers, philosophers, and social historians who remind us that, if we really intend to be serious about what we do, then we must be prepared to read everything.

Ammons, A. R. "A Poem is a Walk." *Epoch*, 18 (Fall 1968), 114-119.
Barzun, Jacques. *A Stroll With William James*. New York: Harper and Row, 1983.
Benson, Herbert, M. D., with Miriam Z. Klipper. *The Relaxation Response*. New York: Avon, 1975; London: Collins, 1976.
Bly, Robert. "The Three Brains." In *The New Naked Poetry*, ed. Stephen Berg and Robert Mezey. Indianapolis: Bobbs-Merrill, 1976.

Cauvin, Jean-Pierre. "Introduction: The Poethics [sic] of André Breton." In *Poems of André Breton: A Bilingual Anthology*, trans. and ed. Jean-Pierre Cauvin and Mary Ann Caws. Austin: University of Texas Press, 1983.

Davie, Donald. *Trying to Explain*. Ann Arbor: University of Michigan Press, 1979.

Debicki, Andrew. *Poetry of Discovery: The Spanish Generation of 1956-71*. Lexington: The University Press of Kentucky, 1982.

Drake, Barbara. *Writing Poetry*. New York: Harcourt Brace Jovanovich, 1983.

Fitzgerald, F. Scott. "The Rich Boy." In *The Literature of the United States*, ed. Walter Blair *et al.* 3rd ed. Vol. III. Glenview, Illinois and London: Scott, Foresman, 1969.

Freud, Sigmund. "General Introduction" to *Psychoanalysis*. In *The Standard Edition of the Complete Psychological Works of Sigmund Freud*, trans. from the German under the general editorship of James Strachey, in collaboration with Anna Freud, assisted by Alix Strachey and Alan Tyson. London: The Hogarth Press and The Institute of Psycho-Analysis, 1957.

Fussell, Paul, Jr. *Poetic Meter and Poetic Form*. New York: Random House, 1965.

Kinnell, Galway. "The Poetics of the Physical World." In *The New Naked Poetry*, ed. Stephen Berg and Robert Mezey. Indianapolis: Bobbs-Merrill, 1976.

Koch, Kenneth. *Wishes, Lies, and Dreams: Teaching Children to Write Poetry*. New York: Harper and Row, 1970.

Kumin, Maxine. "Closing the Door." In *To Make a Prairie: Essays on Poets, Poetry, and Country Living*. Ann Arbor: University of Michigan Press, 1979.

Kunitz, Stanley. "A Kind of Order." In *A Kind of Order*. Boston: Little, Brown, 1975.

Levine, Philip. *Don't Ask*. Ann Arbor: University of Michigan Press, 1981.

Nemerov, Howard. "Poetry and Meaning." In *Figures of Thought: Speculations on the Meaning of Poetry and Other Essays*. Boston: Godine, 1978.

Rinaldi, Nicholas. *We Have Lost Our Fathers and Other Poems*. Orlando: The University Presses of Florida, 1982.

Sontag, Susan. "Against Interpretation." In *Against Interpretation and Other Essays*. New York: Farrar, Straus and Giroux, 1966; London: Eyre and Spottiswoode, 1967.

Thompson, Lawrance, and R. H. Winnick. *Robert Frost: A Biography*. New York: Holt, Rinehart and Winston, 1981.

Wright, James. "Spring Images." In *The Branch Will Not Break: Poems*. Middletown: Wesleyan University Press, 1963; London: Longmans, 1963.

Photo by Bob O'Lary

About the Author

David Kirby is a Johns Hopkins Ph.D. who is now Professor of English at Florida State University in Tallahassee. His latest poetry collection is *Sarah Bernhardt's Leg* (Cleveland State University Poetry Center), of which reviewers have said: "In poem after poem, the reach of imagination and its freewheeling grasp of image and idea allow this poet to spin off lengthy sentences with far-reaching narrative range" (*Choice*), and "Kirby demonstrates an often neglected way in which the imagination engages itself with the world" (*Library Journal*). Among his many awards is a fellowship from the National Endowment for the Arts.